STUDIES IN HISTORY, ECONOMICS AND PUBLIC LAW

Edited by the
**FACULTY OF POLITICAL SCIENCE
OF COLUMBIA UNIVERSITY**

NUMBER 465

THE DEVELOPMENTS OF CONGRESSIONAL INVESTIGATIVE POWER

BY

M. NELSON McGEARY

THE DEVELOPMENTS

OF

CONGRESSIONAL

INVESTIGATIVE POWER

BY

M. NELSON McGEARY

1966

OCTAGON BOOKS, INC.

New York

Reprinted 1966
by special arrangement with Columbia University Press

OCTAGON BOOKS, INC.
175 FIFTH AVENUE
NEW YORK, N. Y. 10010

LIBRARY OF CONGRESS CATALOG CARD NUMBER: 66-18040

Printed in U.S.A. by
NOBLE OFFSET PRINTERS, INC.
NEW YORK 3, N. Y.

PREFACE

THE process of government is always changing. The alterations may take place so slowly as to be almost imperceptible, but new techniques in the methods of governing are continually developing as new problems present themselves or as it becomes desirable or necessary for government to make adjustments in the face of political, economic, or social transformations.

The purpose of the present study is to re-examine one small phase of the national government in the United States—the Congressional investigation. Although a few articles have appeared in recent years on this subject, no book-length study has been published since 1929. Indeed, most of the previous literature on the subject was written in the " twenties " at a time when the emphasis of investigations was on the supervision of the Executive. The succeeding economic depression coupled with the emergence of the New Deal—when, for the first time since investigations were well publicized, a strong party majority, presidentially led, was committed to a program of social change—seems to give a somewhat different perspective to investigations. The legal status of these inquiries also is examined in the light of the decisions of the courts in the past decade.

I cannot over-emphasize my appreciation of Professor Arthur W. Macmahon's help in bringing this work to the point of publication. The inspiration for the undertaking first came from him, and he has given many hours to supervising the study. Professors Lindsay Rogers, Schuyler C. Wallace, and Joseph P. Chamberlain all read the manuscript in its entirety and made helpful suggestions as to both the content and the style. Professor Noel T. Dowling's comments on Chapter V enabled me to avoid several pitfalls in the discussion of the legal aspects of the subject. All these men may, of course, disclaim any responsibility for the statements, conclusions, and errors in this book. I must add that the writing of this work would have been impossible without the help of a large number of the members of Congressional investigating committees, members of regulatory commissions, and members of the investigating staffs employed by these committees and commissions; I am grateful to them for information and for advice.

Professor Frederic A. Ogg has been kind enough to allow me to use material which I included in an article in the *American Political Science Review* of August 1937.

Mrs. C. A. Stewart was of marked assistance in working out the details of publication.

And finally, I was fortunate in being able to learn the value of a wife's aid and encouragement.

M. Nelson McGeary.

State College, Pa.

CONTENTS

CHAPTER I

INTRODUCTORY

Since 1792, when Congressional investigations first appeared above the legislative horizon, they have illuminated many a dark problem, lighted scores of shadowy corners, and sometimes disclosed carefully hidden skeletons. But the record is by no means impeccable. Not uncommonly investigations have become so overcast by clouds of their own making as to nullify every worthwhile accomplishment. The variations in the purposes, procedures, and results of Congressional investigations have led to wide divergence in the opinions of critics, even among legislators themselves. Some have contended, like Senator Nye, that " Out of practically every investigation there comes legislation improving the security of the Government and the people against selfishness and greed." [1] Others, like Representative Warren, have said : " In my opinion 95 per cent of these investigations are absolutely worthless and nothing has been accomplished by them." [2]

Until the last decade no extended study had been made of Congressional investigations as a whole. The subject was covered, however, in two full-length studies,[3] published in 1928 and 1929. Both writers carefully traced the development of the investigating power from its beginnings and both drew conclusions as to its future.

The past decade, however, has witnessed broad transformations in both the economic and political settings. The nation has toppled from previously unmatched heights of prosperity to the bottom of a depression judged by many as the worst in history. At the same time the governmental reins passed from

[1] Radio address of May 23, 1933, reproduced in *Congressional Record,* 73d Cong., 1st Sess., p. 4182.

[2] *Congressional Record,* 74th Cong., 1st Sess., p. 6339, April 24, 1935.

[3] Ernest J. Eberling, *Congressional Investigations* (New York, 1928) ; Marshall E. Dimock, *Congressional Investigating Committees* (Baltimore, Johns Hopkins Press, 1929).

a party leaning toward the status quo to a majority committed to social change. Meanwhile, Congress, especially the Senate, has conducted inquiries in rapid succession. Several questions arise, therefore, as to the current position of investigations. Have the economic and political alterations affected the process? Have shifts in emphasis occurred? Are the previously noted defects being remedied? Has the legal status of the investigating bodies undergone any change?

The present study is limited in its scope. The " Congressional investigations " which are treated are the inquiries that are conducted, in pursuance of a resolution or statute, by Congressional committees or subcommittees. Standing committees have come to be preferred although select or special committees are frequently employed. During the ten years covered by the seventy-first to the seventy-fifth Congresses inclusive, one hundred and forty-six inquiries by committees were authorized, eighty-four by the Senate, fifty by the House, and twelve by the two houses combined. Of these, eighty-nine investigations were made by standing committees or subcommittees, and fifty-seven by select committees.

CONGRESS HAS OTHER METHODS OF OBTAINING INFORMATION. While this study is primarily concerned with investigations carried on by committees under resolutions or statutes, it should be borne in mind that Congress has other formal ways of obtaining facts. In the first place, interrogations may be conducted before the bar of either house. This practice, rarely employed, is generally used as a last resort to combat relatively serious cases of recalcitrancy before Congressional committees.[4] Thus, William P. MacCracken, on the recommendation of the Senate committee investigating air mail contracts,[5] was ordered to appear before the bar of the Senate after permitting the removal from his files of papers subpoenaed by the committee.[6]

[4] Committees have no power to punish.

[5] S. Res. 349, 72d Cong., 2d Sess., February 25, 1933.

[6] See *infra*, p. 109.

More common are investigations by standing committees conducted on their own initiative without an authorizing resolution. These inquiries, which go on steadily during the sessions of Congress, are an important source of information to the legislators. Investigations of this type are often held in connection with proposed bills, but they are not limited to this purpose. For example, an inquiry into charges of corruption in the Department of Commerce was undertaken solely on the vote of the Senate Commerce Committee in June 1935. The accusations were made by E. Y. Mitchell who had been ousted by the President as Assistant Secretary of Commerce after refusing to resign. In opening the hearings,[7] Chairman Copeland explained: " Yesterday the committee on Commerce voted unanimously, and it was decided to ask Mr. Mitchell to come before the committee and make any statement that he cares to make. We have read the statements in the newspapers, but it is the conception of the committee that it is this committee which parallels the activities of the Department of Commerce, and therefore that this committee should be fully informed if there are irregularities—if there are any defects in the operation of the Department, that we should be the first to be advised." [8] Standing committees wishing to compel testimony, however, must obtain authority from the House or Senate, as the case may be.

[7] Hearings of the Senate Committee on Commerce (June 19, 20, 21, 1935), 74th Cong., 1st Sess., on *Alleged Irregularities in the Department of Commerce.*

[8] After three days of testimony Mr. Mitchell was unable to gain much sympathy for his points. See his volume, *Kicked In and Kicked Out of the President's Little Cabinet* (Washington, The Andrew Jackson Press, 1936), especially chap. XXV entitled "Chairman Royal S. Copeland Applies 'Whitewash'". Mr. Mitchell complains: " I was the only witness subpoenaed (Secretary Roper and six of his aides were the other witnesses) and *I was the only witness sworn!* . . . Chairman Copeland treated me like a prisoner on the dock. . . . (There were) three Hearings covering only ten hours, when a Hearing really intended to develop the facts would have required as many months. At the close of these brief sessions he announced to the press, ' Mitchell's charges have disappeared into thin air.' "

But Congress may delegate to others the task of investigating. Resolutions or bills may request administrative agencies to conduct special inquiries. The Federal Trade Commission, for example, has continually been asked to investigate. Although there has been a waning use of this agency, some of its inquiries have been highly significant, especially the investigation of the electric and gas public utility corporations [9] begun in 1928 and not closed until 1936. From month to month during most of that time the Commission submitted to the Senate a total of seven exhibit volumes and eighty-four interim reports which illustrated the propaganda techniques of the utilities and pointed out a long list of questionable practices.[10] Primarily recommending taxation and direct prohibitive legislation, the reports helped to incite the enactment of the public utility act of 1935.[11]

The departments are also asked to make inquiries, although less frequently than are the independent commissions. The Senate, for instance, requested the Secretary of Agriculture to investigate the practicability and the advantages to agriculture of using alcohol, manufactured from corn and other farm products, in motor fuel.[12] Within this category also fall simple requests to administrative officers for information which they may have available. Such demands, on the one hand, may be friendly acts effecting cohesion between the executive and the legislature, as when the Senate asked the Administrator of Public Works for information concerning the organization, policies, and program of the Public Works Administration; [13] or, on the other hand, may amount to an attack, as when a resolution sought information on the past and current business

[9] S. Res. 83, 70th Cong., 1st Sess., February 13, 1928.

[10] S. Doc. 92, 70th Cong., 1st Sess., parts 1 to 84.

[11] 49 Stat. 831.

[12] S. Res. 65, 73d Cong., 1st Sess., May 2, 1933.

[13] S. Res. 190, 73d Cong., 2d Sess., February 15, 1934. The resolution was introduced by Senator LaFollette who, on April 11, introduced a bill to provide additional appropriations for public works, S. 3348.

connections of the employees of the National Recovery Administration.[14] The immediate stimulus of the latter resolution was a newspaper article published on February 9, 1934, by Drew Pearson and Robert Allen [15] which led Senator Nye to state in debate: " The contention has been made and repeated many times that N. R. A. is . . . chock full of representatives and spokesmen of big business institutions, and that through their activity and their control codes are being adopted and codes are being enforced which are very injurious to the smaller units of business throughout the country." Although General Johnson of the N. R. A. had promised " to provide the information even without a resolution if Nye asks for it," Senator Robinson, the Majority Leader, at first refused to allow the request to pass by unanimous consent, insisting that it be routed through the Finance Committee. After one day's delay it was adopted with minor amendments added by the committee.

Congressional delegation of the power to inquire also may be made to a commission composed of individuals who are in no way connected with the government. Thus, Congress in 1912 created a Commission on Industrial Relations to inquire into the general conditions of labor and the relations between employers and employees.[16] The act directed the President to appoint nine commissioners, no less than three to represent employers and the same number to represent organized labor. A more recent example of an extra-governmental commission was the National Commission on Law Observance and Enforcement (Wickersham Commission) composed of eleven laymen, which was created by President Hoover after Congress had appropriated $250,000 for a study of law enforcement.[17] In this instance Congress did not specify how the investigation should be made, but allowed the President to use his discretion.

[14] S. Res. 175, 73d Cong., 2d Sess., February 21, 1934.

[15] *Congressional Record*, 73d Cong., 2d Sess., p. 2832.

[16] 37 Stat. 415.

[17] 45 Stat. 1613, March 4, 1929.

The Executive has, on the whole, made rather wide use of this "Royal Commission" device,[18] but Congress has been reluctant to adopt it.

When the General Accounting Office was established in 1921, it took over the auditing operations of the Treasury Department. Congress apparently expected the Comptroller General to serve as a useful informant. One of his functions was to be the making of investigations for and reports to Congress on violations of the law in financial matters.[19] To carry out this mandate he was given "a comprehensive power of investigation . . . with the right of access to all official records, such as congressional investigating committees might have." But the results have been less than were anticipated. At least one student of the subject argues that this "main feature of the act has broken down completely" and that "Congress has not the information adequate to the discharge of" its duties.[20]

An additional source of information is the Court of Claims. Sprinkled here and there in the activities of Congress are resolutions asking this Court to "hear, determine, and render judgment" on claims against the government.[21] The recommendations of the Court carry important weight in the final Congressional decisions.

Congress also utilizes various hybrids of the above methods. A Congressional committee may make such an extended use of

[18] On occasion, Congress provides funds for an investigation which the President has already instigated. Thus, when the House began debate on an appropriation of $50,000 to "cover any expenses which may be incurred by the President, through such methods as he may employ, in making a study and report on the conservation and administration of the public domain" (46 Stat. 153), twenty-one of the twenty-five members of a commission had already been designated by President Hoover. *Congressional Record*, 71st Cong., 2d Sess., p. 2243, January 23, 1930.

[19] 42 Stat. 20, sec. 312.

[20] Harvey C. Mansfield, in President's Committee on Administrative Management, *Report with Special Studies* (1937), pp. 190-1. See *infra*, p. 141.

[21] An example was S. Res. 147, 75th Cong., 1st Sess., June 28, 1937, which referred a bill "for the relief of the First, Second, and Third National Steamship Cos." to the Court of Claims for findings of fact.

experts as to approximate an investigation by an extra-govern-mental commission. The National Monetary Commission of 1908,[22] for instance, was composed of eighteen members of Congress, but, conducting only a few hearings, it relied to a considerable extent on a wealth of monographs published under the auspices of the Commission. The report with the substan-tiating material, contained in twenty-three volumes,[23] influ-enced the shaping of the federal reserve act of 1913.

A unique arrangement for the investigation of the concen-tration of economic power was provided in 1938 in a Tem-porary National Economic Committee[24] composed of three Senators, three Representatives, and one expert each from the Treasury, Justice, Labor, and Commerce Departments, the Securities and Exchange Commission and the Federal Trade Commission.[25]

This tabulation of fact-finding devices[26] does not take into account the many sources from which Congress may obtain information informally or without assuming the initiative. For example, facts are supplied to the legislators by the Presi-dent and the members of the administrative establishment, and by lobbyists, as well as by such diverse sources as the news-papers and the Legislative Reference Service.

MANY PROPOSED INVESTIGATIONS ARE THROTTLED. Not-withstanding the authorization in each Congress of inquiries by committees into a wide variety of subjects, and despite an absence of effective cloture in the Senate which induces the ratification of the investigations sponsored by a minority, many

[22] 35 Stat. 552. See *infra*, p. 130.

[23] *Publications of the National Monetary Commission* (1911-1912); the Commission's report is also found in S. Doc. 243, 62d Cong., 2d Sess.

[24] 52 Stat. 705, June 16, 1938. See *infra*, pp. 41 and 146.

[25] The War Policies Commission of 1930 also was composed of both legislators and administrators. This Commission, which studied the procedure to be followed in equalizing the burdens of war, was made up of four Senators, four Representatives, and six cabinet members (46 Stat. 825).

[26] See Chapter VI for a discussion of some of the considerations involved when Congress chooses an investigative device.

resolutions fail to obtain approval. In both the Senate and the House more investigations are killed than are accepted. Often they deal with minor subjects and are proposed, with little serious hope of passage, only for political reasons. Thus, the introduction of a resolution may produce newspaper copy desirable to a Congressman. Or it may merely convey disapproval; the preamble of a resolution often serves as a convenient platform for the expression of opinions. Other proposed investigations are genuine attempts at action, but are doomed to oblivion. The majority of the resolutions die in committee.[27] Once reported, however, they are generally enacted; few suffer an adverse vote on the floor. Random examples in the seventy-fifth Congress of those failing to pass beyond the committee stage were: in the Senate, investigations of the General Motors corporation, the government's purchases of silver, the government of the District of Columbia, the Resettlement Administration (four separate resolutions), and the charges made in a volume entitled "The Nine Old Men"; in the House, inquiries into the prices of automobiles, public opinion polls, the radio industry, the American Bar Association, the brewers, the motion picture industry, the baseball "trust", and the Federal Communications Commission (three resolutions).[28]

[27] This is, of course, also true of other types of resolutions and bills.

[28] The House Committee on Rules, because nearly all resolutions providing for investigations are referred to it, is able to pigeon-hole most investigations. An analysis of the resolutions introduced in the lower chamber in one session of Congress (the first session of the seventy-fifth) indicates the control which this committee exercises. Of the seventy-three resolutions introduced in the House suggesting inquiries to be conducted by committees of the House or by joint committees, seventy were referred to the Rules Committee. The committee reported back nine resolutions, of which six were passed, one was rejected, and two were laid on the table. In addition, the committee reported and the House approved S. Con. Res. 18, which provided for an investigation by a joint committee; and reported a special order (H. Res. 226) for the consideration of S. J. Res. 155 (50 Stat. 253, June 11, 1937) which created a joint committee to investigate the evasion of income taxes. The two remaining inquiries of the session were approved when resolutions were brought up by unanimous consent just before Congress adjourned on August 21 (H. Res. 332 and H. Res. 339, August 20 and 21, 1937).

Occasionally a subject may be so delicate as to discourage any concerted effort toward investigation. Thus, the activities of labor, particularly organized labor, have been singularly free of probing. This observation is not intended to imply that an investigation has been or is desirable. It is noteworthy, however, considering the Congressional propensity for such activities, that labor groups, on the whole, have escaped inquiry. Both the Senate and the House appear to respect a political force which, although it never has been fully coordinated, is nevertheless powerful. Not only has labor avoided an inquisitorial investigation, but few such inquiries are proposed. President Hoover's term witnessed none. Less surprising, perhaps, in a New Deal atmosphere of betterment for labor, was the continued dearth after 1933 of suggestions for the probing of labor. In 1937, following the spread of the sitdown strike, a handful of resolutions aimed at general or specific conditions originating from strikes were proposed in the House,[29] but each, with one exception, progressed no further than the Committee on Rules. The exception was the closest step during the last decade toward the authorization by Congress of an investigation of labor. Representative Dies, because " an epidemic of sitdown strikes is sweeping the Nation and threatening the very foundations of orderly government," introduced a two-edged resolution [30] authorizing an inquiry into sitdown strikes and their causes and the measures taken by local communities to handle such situations. In a House described as " uproarious ", and featured by bitter debate, the anti-New Dealers favored the resolution in a desire to embarrass an Administration sympathetic to labor. Indeed, rumor accused

[29] No resolutions for investigating the sitdown strikes were introduced in the Senate. The Senate approved, by 75 to 3, a concurrent resolution (not approved by the House) which stated in part: " That it is the sense of the Congress that the so-called sitdown strike is illegal and contrary to sound public policy ". The resolution also condemned the "industrial spy system" and other "unfair labor practices" on the part of employers. *Congressional Record*, 75th Cong., 1st Sess., p. 3248, April 7, 1937.

[30] H. Res. 162, 75th Cong., 1st Sess.

the Republicans and insurgent Democrats of forcing it to the
floor past napping Administration spokesmen. The test vote,
which was made on ordering the previous question on the
resolution, brought 150 yeas and 236 nays.[31] By unanimous
consent, the resolution then was laid on the table.[32]

Exemplary of an Administration's [33] resistance to inquiry,
only temporarily successful, were the rebuffs to the repeated
attempts at an investigation of the administration of relief.
As might be expected in connection with a money-spending
project of this nature, scores of charges were made in Congress
pertaining to mismanagement. The chief accusations concerned
the use of relief funds by administrators to influence votes.
Undeniably, some charges were exaggerated and were made
for the principal purpose of embarrassing the party in power,
but undoubtedly, on the other hand, political maneuvering had
crept into the management of relief at some points. More debatable than its presence were the degree to which it had flour-
ished, and the level of its entrance. The desirability of an investigation was suggested, if for no other reason, by the results of an American Institute of Public Opinion (Gallup) poll
which asked a national cross section of voters: " In your
opinion, does politics play a part in the handling of relief in
your locality?" Sixty-five per cent answered " yes ", eighteen
" no ", and seventeen per cent had no opinion. Even among
those on relief, forty-nine per cent answered " yes ".[34] This

[31] *Congressional Record*, 75th Cong., 1st Sess., p. 3301, April 8, 1937.

[32] A year later the House adopted a Dies resolution directing an investigation of " un-American " activities (H. Res. 282, 75th Cong., 3d Sess., May
26, 1938). In an atmosphere of criticism of the New Deal, the committee,
with Mr. Dies as chairman, turned a portion of its attention to the sitdown strikes.

[33] The term "Administration" has at least two meanings. It may refer
merely to those who execute the laws in a routine way. But it is used here
in the political sense to include the President and those who work with him
in formulating as well as carrying out general governmental policies.
Thus used, it is capitalized in this study.

[34] *Washington Post*, April 25, 1936; reproduced in *Congressional Record*,
74th Cong., 2d Sess., p. 6414.

poll, conducted in April 1936, was followed by another in 1938 which posed the question: " Do you think the Roosevelt Administration is using the Works Progress Administration to elect New Deal candidates to Congress?" To this, fifty-four percent replied " yes " and forty-six percent " no ".[35]

Regardless of the extent of the political manipulation connected with the management of relief, however, the Administration stood to suffer from a Congressional investigation.[36] During the second session of the seventy-fourth Congress (a Presidential election year) [37] no fewer than five resolutions, three in the House and two in the Senate, proposed investigations into the general administration of relief, or into waste, delays in payments, or politics.[38] All were blocked in committees, although one showed some signs of life. Senator Davis, because " the Works Progress Administration is surrounded by an air of mystery and secrecy," sought a general investigation of the agency.[39] The Committee on Expenditures in the Executive Departments approved and added the Federal Relief Administration to the resolution, but the Committee to Audit and Control the Contingent Expenses of the Senate,

[35] *New York Times*, June 19, 1938.

[36] Congressional investigations may, of course, aid as well as curb an Administration. This phase of the subject is treated in Chapter II. See *infra*, p. 34.

[37] No opposition was offered to a resolution adopted in 1935 which asked for a report from Administrator Harry Hopkins on the methods of distribution and the amounts allotted to the states by the Federal Emergency Relief Administration (S. Res. 115, 74th Cong., 1st Sess.).

[38] One resolution of inquiry (H. Res. 493), also aimed at embarrassment, was defeated by a roll call vote of 243 to 98. It requested the President to transmit to the House a copy of a report, rumored to be critical, submitted by Hugh Johnson upon the completion of his term as administrator of the W.P.A. in New York City. The resolution was reported adversely by the Committee on Expenditures in the Executive Departments following a statement by Harry Hopkins that " In this memorandum are a number of references to individuals and agencies outside of the W.P.A. which are of a private and confidential nature." *Congressional Record*, 74th Cong., 2d Sess., p. 6370, April 29, 1936.

[39] S. Res. 243, 74th Cong., 2d Sess.

voting apparently on partisan lines, refused to bring it to the floor. The Senator from Pennsylvania, blocked in this path, then offered a resolution of inquiry requesting information "denied to the General Assembly of Pennsylvania," concerning the personnel of the W. P. A. and the disbursements in Pennsylvania.[40] Asking unanimous consent to proceed to the immediate consideration of the resolution, he was again rebuffed, this time by the objection of Majority Leader Robinson. In the same Congress, however, one concession was made to the critics in the Senate. In accordance with custom, a select committee had been suggested to investigate the campaign expenditures by and for the candidates in the 1936 elections for President, Vice-President, and the Senate.[41] Following the vote of approval, Minority Leader McNary, speaking for Senator Hastings who was absent, promised a motion to reconsider. Several days later, on the motion of Senator Robinson— who explained "We have discussed the matter and have agreed upon an amendment"—the committee was further directed to investigate "not only as to the subscriptions of money and expenditures thereof but as to the use of any other means of influence, including the promise or use of patronage." The committee, however, found no influence by relief administrators worthy of condemnation in its report.[42]

The barrages upon the administration of relief continued in the seventy-fifth Congress. Three House resolutions died in the Rules Committee; two Senate proposals fared no better. By June 1938, however, when Congress was considering a new relief appropriation measure,[43] an anti-New Deal movement concentrated on prevention in place of investigation. Senator Hatch, for one, offered an amendment to the effect that "No person employed in any administrative capacity by any agency of the Federal Government whose compensation, or any part

[40] S. Res. 314, 74th Cong., 2d Sess.
[41] S. Res. 225, 74th Cong., 2d Sess., April 1, 1936.
[42] S. Rept. 151, 75th Cong., 1st Sess., March 4, 1937.
[43] 52 Stat. 809.

thereof, is paid from funds appropriated by title I of this act shall use his official authority or influence for the purpose of interfering with or influencing a convention, a primary, or other election, or affecting the results thereof. Any such person shall retain the right to vote as he pleases and to express his opinions on all political subjects, but shall take no active part in political management or in political campaigns." [44] The penalty for nonobservance was removal from office. Just enough stalwarts of the Administration rallied behind the Majority Leader to defeat the proposition by a vote of 37 to 40. The next day, the line-ups remained approximately intact when, by 33 to 35, the Senate disposed of Senator Austin's amendment which sought the same results but which provided penalties of a fine and imprisonment for political activities.

The upshot of these reversals was a renewed insistence on an investigation. A resolution introduced by ten Senators, including wheelhorses as well as critics of the Administration,[45] provided for an inquiry into the alleged use of relief and work relief funds for political purposes.[46] For the Administration to stem the tide any longer seemed inadvisable if not impossible, but the defense did not completely surrender. The Senate adopted an amendment, suggested by the Contingent Expenses Committee, which struck out all after the resolving clause and transferred the responsibility for detecting and reporting politics in relief to the customary committee, already established, on the 1938 campaign expenditures. As revised, therefore, the resolution provided that " the special committee authorized to be appointed by Senate Resolution 283 . . . is hereby directed to make in addition to any investigation which it is directed to make by such resolution, a specific investigation with respect to whether or not any funds appropriated by the Congress (whether for expenditure by any department, independent

[44] *Congressional Record*, 75th Cong., 3d Sess., p. 8000, June 2, 1938.

[45] Senators Tydings, Burke, King, Hatch, Adams, McAdoo, Bulkley, George, Wagner, and Gerry.

[46] S. Res. 290, 75th Cong., 3d Sess., June 16, 1938.

agency, or instrumentality of the United States, or by any State or political subdivision of a State or instrumentality of any State or political subdivision thereof) have been spent or are being spent in such manner as to influence votes cast or to be cast in any primary, convention, or election held in 1938 at which a candidate for the Senate is to be nominated or elected." Fifty thousand dollars were granted in addition to the $30,000 already assigned to the committee. Senator Wheeler, although not one of the ten sponsors of the original resolution, was especially emphatic in denouncing the revision. To him it was meaningless to authorize an investigation as to " whether or not any funds appropriated by the Congress have been spent or are being spent in such manner as to influence votes." The proof would be too difficult. " I say frankly," he insisted, " that I do not believe the resolution will do a particle of good." Senator Walsh of Massachusetts, a member of the Campaign Expenditures Committee, likewise ventured: " I do not want to commit myself in advance, but I do not know how I am going to get any evidence of money being spent for election purposes. John Brown who is a politician may spend some money, but it will be very difficult to show that he is influencing votes . . . The public believe, and Senators believe . . . that the investigation is to be a wide-open investigation of corruption, inefficiency, dishonesty, mismanagement, and everything else of that kind; but it is not . . . So far as I am concerned, being a member of the committee, I do not want the responsibility on my doorstep." [47] Despite the prophecies of ineffectiveness, however, the committee under Senator Sheppard pursued its inquiry with unforeseen vigor, and, issuing public warnings in all directions, frequently placed Democrat and Republican alike on an embarrassed defensive. And in its final report the committee presented detailed illustrations of " unjustifiable political activity " in several states, to fortify its general conclusion that " funds appropriated by the Con-

[47] *Congressional Record*, 75th Cong., 3d Sess., p. 9559, June 16, 1938.

gress for the relief of those in need and distress have been in many instances diverted from these high purposes to political ends." [48]

In any consideration of the investigations which are stifled, the possible importance of the threat of investigation should not be overlooked. There are no scales with which to measure the unethical and undesirable practices which it may prevent. The fear of publicity through investigation may carry the same restraint as fear of the law. A committee's hearings on a proposed resolution may, therefore, even though the inquiry be smothered, serve as a significant warning. Indeed, they sometimes may be almost indistinguishable, both in their procedure and the effects, from a formally authorized investigation.

THE HOUSE OF REPRESENTATIVES CONTINUES IN A MINOR ROLE. Professor Dimock,[49] among others, showed the Senate to be the more important investigator, whereas in earlier times the House was the leader in this respect. In bringing about this change, the freedom of debate in the Senate, associated with the absence of effective cloture, afforded a fulcrum for leverage which drew its real power from the overrepresentation of the agrarian sections.[50] It is interesting to note that the Sen-

[48] S. Rept. 1, 76th Cong., 1st Sess., January 3, 1939. While it is still too early to evaluate the long time effects on relief of the committee's work, it may have laid the groundwork for additional investigations and induced remedies to be applied from both within and without the administration. Thus, an appropriation for relief (H. J. Res. 83, 76th Cong., 1st Sess.) which was approved a month after the submission of the committee's report, declared a number of specified political activities in connection with relief to be unlawful. Moreover, the House, on March 27, approved, 351 to 27, a resolution (H. Res. 130, 76th Cong., 1st Sess.) directing the Committee on Appropriations to conduct "a thorough investigation and study of the Works Progress Administration and the administration of laws, regulations, and orders administered by it." Although the report of the Sheppard committee did not hold Administrator Harry Hopkins responsible for the activities which it condemned, it was used later in January as a weapon by those opposed to his confirmation by the Senate as Secretary of Commerce. He was confirmed, however, on January 23, by a vote of 58 to 27.

[49] Op. cit.

[50] See Lindsay Rogers, The American Senate (New York, A. A. Knopf, 1926), p. 93 ff. and chap. VI.

ate's role continued predominant after 1933 when the emphasis of investigations changed from checking the Administration to collaboration with the Administration.[51] Senators more often than not obtain approval for resolutions by unanimous consent with little or no explanation or debate.

But the upper house leads not only in quantity; most genuinely significant investigations are mothered by "the most powerful upper chamber in the world."

[51] See *infra*, p. 39.

CHAPTER II

PURPOSES OF INVESTIGATIONS

CLASSIFICATION OF CONGRESSIONAL INVESTIGATIONS. The primary tasks of modern legislative assemblies may be arranged in four classes. First, but not necessarily foremost, is the function of law making. At least equally important is the responsibility of supervising the executive; the legislature in this role may be compared to a board of directors of a business corporation which, at least theoretically, endeavors to hold " administrative officers to a due accountability for the manner in which they perform their duties." [1] A third legislative office, broad in its implications, involves activities as an organ of public opinion; a law-making body may serve as a national forum for the expression,[2] formulation, or moulding of opinion. The remaining function, which may be termed membership, concerns internal matters, especially the judging of the qualifications and conduct of the delegates to the legislative assembly.

Congress, in the performance of each of these responsibilities, places considerable reliance on inquiries. A convenient classification of investigations, therefore, can be drawn on the basis of Congressional functions. It should be noted, however, that it is idle to seek a rigid segregation. A neat separation of all investigations into four classes is beset with difficulty. Few inquiries are confined strictly to one purpose. An overlapping of motives is not uncommon; to single out one as transcending all others is sometimes to risk a distortion of emphasis.

(1) Investigations to Assist Congress in Legislating. It is probably safe to say that the bulk of investigations of the past ten years were conducted for the chief purpose of obtaining information to help Congress in drafting laws. The presence

---

[1] W. F. Willoughby, *Principles of Legislative Organization and Administration* (Washington, The Brookings Institution, 1934), p. 157.

[2] This expression of opinion at least involves the voicing of grievances.

of a specific legislative intent at the beginning of an investigation is not essential to the inclusion of the inquiry in this category; the investigation may be made for the purpose of determining whether any legislation is desirable.[3] The more spectacular inquiries of recent years, with few exceptions, fall within this classification. A few conspicuous examples of investigations calculated to assist Congress in drafting legislation were those into stock exchanges and banking,[4] the munitions industry,[5] railroad financing,[6] and the concentration of economic power.[7] In many instances the moulding of public opinion forms an important collateral aim of the investigations in this category. Indeed, " social leverage " frequently is essential if statutory additions or revisions are to be accomplished. The Senate investigation of the munitions industry, for example, was, in the course of its hearings, deeply concerned with the informing function, although the paramount purpose of those in charge probably was the enactment of statutes.

(2) Supervisory Investigations. Congress, in meeting the responsibilities of a " board of directors," works without such tools as the British question-time or the French interpellation and parliamentary commissions. The separation of powers and the fixed Executive terms help to make control sporadic and relatively difficult if not always ineffectual. In place of the devices of parliamentary government, therefore, the Congressional inquiry has been an important factor in the legislative supervision of administrative officers. The underlying motives of investigations within this classification may range from a deliberate attack to an ascertainment of the needs of the executive departments. The attacks may, moreover, be separated into two groups. The first group comprises the investigations

[3] See Chapter V for a discussion of some of the legal aspects of investigations.

[4] S. Res. 84, 72d Cong., 1st Sess., March 4, 1932.

[5] S. Res. 206, 73d Cong., 2d Sess., April 12, 1934.

[6] S. Res. 71, 74th Cong., 1st Sess., May 20, 1935.

[7] 52 Stat. 705, June 16, 1938.

of specific accusations of misfeasance or maladministration. The second includes the inquiries which are sponsored by legislators who disagree with the policy of the Administration or who charge a general administrative inefficiency. Roughly a third of the total Congressional inquiries within recent years may be termed supervisory. Those probes designed to embarrass or to censure the Administration to any appreciable extent have been scarce, which is, as will be seen, in contrast to the previous decade. Indeed, the Senate's investigators only mildly attacked the Hoover and Roosevelt régimes. The most direct censure of administrators came after the seventy-fifth Congress when a House committee led by Representative Dies,[8] a Texas Democrat, attempted to discredit some segments of the Roosevelt Administration by suggestions of communist infiltrations.

The investigations of charges of specific maladministration were also infrequent. One illustration of a comparatively gentle assault followed the airplane crash in which Senator Cutting was killed. When the Senate ordered an investigation of the causes of the wreck,[9] the facts brought out in the public hearings led the committee to find fault with the Bureau of Air Commerce of the Department of Commerce and to recommend an overhauling of its personnel.[10] The reverberations continued until the resignation on February 25, 1937 of the director of the Bureau, which at least indirectly was related to the disclosures.

At the opposite end of the scale are a limited number of investigations, readily classifiable as aids to law making, which, because they aim to weigh proposals by administrators for Congressional assistance in improving the execution of the existing law, may also be catalogued as supervisory inquiries.

[8] H. Res. 282, 75th Cong., 3d Sess., May 26, 1938. H. Rept. 2, 76th Cong., 1st Sess., January 3, 1939.

[9] S. Res. 146, 74th Cong., 1st Sess., June 7, 1935.

[10] S. Rept. 2455, 74th Cong., 2d Sess., June 20, 1936; and S. Rept. 185, 75th Cong., 1st Sess., March 17, 1937.

For example, a joint Congressional committee conducted a study of income tax avoidance when the results of defects in the law were pointed out by the President. A letter from the Secretary of the Treasury to President Roosevelt on May 29, 1937 recapitulated eleven methods of evasion of the current income tax law. This "preliminary" report followed an investigation by a Treasury Department "surprised and disturbed by the failure of the receipts from the income tax on March 15 to measure up to the budget estimates." In the opinion of the Secretary, the conditions disclosed were so serious as to call for "more than the usual examination and audit by the Treasury." The President, therefore, in a special message on the subject appealed for Congress "to give to the Treasury all authority necessary to expand and complete the present preliminary investigation, including, of course, full authority to summon witnesses and compel their testimony."[11] The response was speedy. But Congress, ever jealous of its power to investigate, did not choose to delegate. Only a few moments after the reading of the message, the Senate unanimously approved a resolution offered by the chairman of the Finance Committee providing for an inquiry by a joint committee of six members from each chamber.[12] Section 5 of the resolution, which authorized the Treasury Department to investigate for the committee, was probably unique: "The joint committee may authorize any one or more officers or employees of the Treasury Department to conduct any part of such investigation on behalf of the committee, and for such purpose any person so authorized may hold such hearings and require by subpoena or otherwise the attendance of such witnesses and the production of such books, papers, and documents, administer such oaths, and take such testimony as the committee may authorize. In any such case subpoenas shall be issued under the signature of the chairman of the Joint committee and shall be served by any person designated by him." But the House, even more

11 *Congressional Record*, 75th Cong., 1st Sess., p. 5166, June 1, 1937.
12 50 Stat. 253, June 11, 1937.

cautious than the Senate, agreed with the chairman of its Rules Committee that this provision made " Congress but an empty shell, being used as a cloak " for having " the investigation conducted by the Treasury Department," and amended section 5 to insure that " nothing in this section shall be construed as authorizing a public hearing " by the Department.[13] The Senate soon concurred. After the joint committee's hearings, which were chiefly aimed at publicizing the information unearthed by the Treasury, the committee issued a report [14] that " amply sustained " the Secretary.[15] Legislation designed to plug the loopholes was soon enacted.

Interesting to the observer, both because it was an innovation and because of the possibilities involved in close-range, semi-confidential supervision of the executive, was the provision on August 16, 1935 for a special committee in the Senate [16] to confer with the Secretary of the Treasury regarding the administration and the effect here and abroad of the silver purchase act of 1934.[17] This law, sponsored by Senator Pittman, a representative of Nevada and a spokesman for silver, provided for the purchase by the government of silver until its price reached $1.29 an ounce (the current market price was forty-four cents) or until the monetary value of the silver stocks of the United States reached one-third that of the gold. The act was widely ridiculed as an unfortunate sop to the silver interests over-represented in the Senate. It gave the Secretary of the Treasury power to set the day-to-day price of the metal. At one time when the Treasury was paying approximately seventy-eight cents an ounce, however, the Secretary

[13] *Congressional Record*, 75th Cong., 1st Sess., p. 5460, June 8, 1937.

[14] H. Doc. 337, 75th Cong., 1st Sess., August 5, 1937.

[15] On the other hand, some evidence, brought out in the hearings, of red tape in the Bureau of Internal Revenue doubtless had a bearing on the assignment of Harold N. Graves, an administrative expert of the Treasury, to overhaul the Bureau. *New York Times*, September 20, 1937.

[16] S. Res. 187, 74th Cong., 1st Sess., August 16, 1935.

[17] 48 Stat. 1178.

was reported [18] as professing not to know how or why the price was determined. Moreover, although the Senate's special silver committee was packed with representatives of the silver states,[19] the Secretary had, the report added, suggested that this committee should advise him as to the price they considered proper. The affairs of the committee meanwhile remained a secret. Its secretary, in answer to an inquiry, wrote on March 12, 1937, a year and a half after the creation of the committee: " it has been impossible, so far this session, to call a meeting of this Committee, but it is expected that a meeting will be called in the not far distant future, at which time it is anticipated that a progress report will be formulated and submitted to the Senate." [20] Although the authorizing resolution directed that " the said committee shall report to the Senate as soon as practicable the results of its investigations, together with its recommendations," no report has to date been issued.

Joint action by the Senate and the House brought an important supervisory investigation late in the seventy-fifth Congress. Soon after the creation of the Tennessee Valley Authority in 1933 close observers were aware of frictions among its three directors. Not until five years later, however, did the general public learn of the smoulderings when Arthur E. Morgan, the chairman, complained of his " difficulty " in securing

[18] *Washington Post*, February 18, 1937.

[19] Senator Pittman introduced the resolution and became the committee's chairman.

[20] Letter to the writer. Impelled, perhaps, by the growing criticism of the act and of the secrecy attached to its administration, the committee held the first of a series of public hearings on February 7, 1939. The Senate, in the meantime, had added four members, not identified with the silver bloc, to the committee. The chairman, at the opening of the hearings, stated that " The committee has conferred with the Secretary of the Treasury through the chairman, on several occasions, obtaining information desired by various members of the committee and other Members of the Senate relative to purchases under the act. Meetings have been held at various places in the United States for the purpose of obtaining facts with regard to the production of silver, and matters relating to it. This is the first comprehensive hearing on this subject." The Secretary of the Treasury was the principal witness.

"honesty, openness, decency and fairness in government."[21] The counter thrusts by his fellow board members held that the chairman had "obstructed and sabotaged" the work of the T. V. A. The forces of the Administration and others sympathetic to the Authority were first marshalled to forestall any Congressional investigation. Some well-informed commentators explained the motivation of this defense as a fear, not of any exposure of corruption, but of the ridicule which could result even in the absence of impropriety. Further events, however, made an inquiry inescapable. Chairman Morgan, interrogated on two occasions by President Roosevelt, refused to produce evidence to support his charges, and insisted upon a Congressional investigation. The next defensive move was an effort to authorize an examination by the Federal Trade Commission rather than by a Congressional committee. But a suspicion of the dominance of the Commission by the President, and doubts as to its competence to delve into the affairs of a coordinate administrative agency, led to the naming of a joint committee of five Senators and five Representatives with broad authority to inquire into not only the charges but also the general policies of the Authority, the legitimacy of its yardstick for private power rates, and the efforts of private utility companies to obstruct the project.[22]

The examinations of charges of misconduct where impeachment is being considered may also be tabulated as supervisory investigations.[23] A total of five House resolutions were en-

---

[21] *New York Times*, March 3, 1938.

[22] 52 Stat. 154, April 4, 1938.

[23] Since the impeachment process has been almost entirely confined to judges, a separate classification for this group of inquiries might be justified. A resolution asking the Judiciary Committee to ascertain whether impeachment proceedings are advisable may be referred to that committee for recommendation and thereby may be made the basis for an investigation. Thus, the committee held hearings on H. Res. 67, 76th Cong., 1st Sess., which requested an investigation of Secretary Perkins and also of two other executives in the Department of Labor. The resolution was, however, laid on the table when a unanimous committee, on March 24, reported (H. Rept. 311) it adversely. In the same way, hearings were conducted in

acted asking the Committee on the Judiciary to inquire into the conduct of federal judges.[24] Two judges were impeached, although one was acquitted by the Senate.[25]

(3) Informing Investigations. Previous writers on the subject have not been unmindful of the part played by investigations in assisting Congress with its function of providing a national forum. But this inchoate phase of inquiries has perhaps been insufficiently stressed. The procedure in inquiries belies the suggestion that Congressmen have been unaware of the possibilities, but they have not, when asking for investigations, laid much emphasis on the potentialities of guiding the nation's thinking. Caution may have been prescribed by the judiciary's ratification of investigations on other grounds.[26] Legislators have at times made the point, however, that investigators can help the country to form opinions. Senator McCormick of Illinois clearly expressed the thought when, in offering a resolution directing a probe of railroad strikes,[27] he insisted: " what is needed . . . is some body of men which may bring the facts to public attention. There is no other possible means of mobilizing that public opinion which may induce the men to return to work." Representative Keller re-echoed the view

1932 on H. Res. 92, 72d Cong., 1st Sess., which was directed at the Secretary of the Treasury Andrew W. Mellon; the committee recommended, after Mr. Mellon had been appointed Ambassador to England, that further consideration of the charges be discontinued (H. Rept. 444, 72d Cong.).

24 H. Res. 191, 71st Cong., 2d Sess.; H. Res. 284, 71st Cong., 2d Sess.; H. Res. 239, 72d Cong., 1st Sess.; H. Res. 120, 73d Cong., 1st Sess.; H. Res. 163, 73d Cong., 1st Sess.

25 Harold Louderback, a district judge of California, who was investigated under the authority of H. Res. 239 of the 72d Congress, was impeached for his activities in connection with receiverships, but was acquitted by the Senate on May 24, 1933. The subcommittee investigating (H. Res. 163, 73d Cong.) the conduct of Halsted L. Ritter, a Florida district judge, voted two to one against recommending impeachment, but the full Judiciary Committee, after voting to drop the charges, reversed itself, with the result that the Judge was impeached by the House. The Senate, on April 17, 1936, found him guilty of high crimes and misdemeanors in office.

26 See Chapter V.

27 S. Res. 346, 66th Cong., 2d Sess., April 9, 1920.

when, advocating an inquiry into reorganizations by real estate bondholders,[28] he urged on the members of the House the importance of public knowledge of the facts and emphasized that an investigation would " throw the fear of God into the hearts of those who are robbing the people." Evidence has accumulated to substantiate the conjecture that investigations, to an increasing extent, are devoted to effecting social leverage. Generally, however, the motives are mixed. In most instances, admittedly, the moulding of opinion is collateral to the enactment of law or to supervision. Inquiries are so conducted as to draw the wide attention of Congress, the press, and the public, and to place a strong impetus for action behind recommended legislation. In scattered investigations, however, the swaying of opinion may be the predominant motive. Thus, in 1936 the members of both houses were becoming alarmed at the increasing power and influence of the Townsend movement which aimed at providing all persons over sixty years of age with a pension of two hundred dollars a month. When criticism by economists failed to arrest it, and the movement was becoming politically troublesome, the House resorted to an investigation.[29] Although the Doctor was able to assume a role suggesting martyrdom, his cause probably lost more prestige and following than it gained as a result of the hearings and the prosecution that succeeded his contumacy.[30] Most of the frequent investigations of election campaign expenditures [31] and of lobbying [32] also seem chiefly calculated to stimulate the play of public opinion; activities which are difficult to control by statute are thus held in check to some extent by exposure.

Social leverage received particular attention from the LaFollette committee investigating strike breaking, industrial espion-

[28] H. Res. 412, 73d Cong., 2d Sess., June 15, 1934.

[29] H. Res. 443, 74th Cong., 2d-Sess., March 10, 1936.

[30] See *infra*, p. 112, footnote.

[31] See *infra*, p. 32.

[32] Two of the spectacular investigations of recent years, in addition to other minor inquiries, were concerned with lobbying: S. Res. 20, 71st Cong., 1st Sess., October 1, 1929, and S. Res. 165, 74th Cong., 1st Sess., July 11, 1935.

age, and other infringements of civil liberties.[33] Although the paramount aim of the committee probably was to draft legislation, every effort was made to dramatize the facts and to arouse a body of opinion to action against some of the conditions which were uncovered. The informing function is, as a matter of fact, an important element of practically all investigations. Indeed, were it not a factor, less justification would remain for the average public hearing, since much of the open testimony is taken for the principal purpose of swinging a spotlight on facts already gathered.[34]

(4) Membership Investigations. Both the Senate and the House conduct investigations in pursuance of three expressed or implied powers relating to their own members: judging the " elections, returns, and qualifications ";[35] punishing for disorderly behaviour;[36] and protecting against breaches of immunity or of the dignity of either house. The inquiries in this category form only a fraction of the total. The classification may be dismissed with a few examples of the membership investigations of the past decade.

Outstanding are the habitual select committees appointed in each house to inquire into the campaign expenditures for candidates to the Senate or House, as the case may be. Every fourth year, the expenses for the Presidential and Vice-Presidential nominees are also included. The most far-reaching results from such investigations in recent years probably came from the Senate committee probing the 1926 elections.[37] The information which it unearthed as to lavish expenses in the

[33] S. Res. 266, 74th Cong., 2d Sess., June 6, 1936.

[34] See infra, p. 73.

[35] Art. I, sec. 5, para. I.

[36] Art. I, sec. 5, para. 2.

[37] S. Res. 195, 69th Cong., 1st Sess., May 19, 1926. It is premature to compare the results of the work of the 1938 Senate committee (see supra, p. 19) whose added task of examining the use of federal funds to influence votes gave a supervisory twist to the inquiry.

primaries led to the denial of a seat in the Senate to William S. Vare of Pennsylvania.[38]

Each new Congress has its share of contested seats. The inquiries concerning disputed elections do not, however, require resolutions of authorization. It has become customary to refer such questions to the Committee on Privileges and Elections of the Senate, or to one of the Committees on Elections of the House. When a committee makes its decision, a resolution is introduced declaring the winner. These investigations which are brought about without a resolution are not included in the present study. In a few exceptional cases, however, resolutions do stimulate inquiries into elections. For example, a specific authorization and $40,000 was given to the Committee on Privileges and Elections to determine " whether J. Thomas Heflin or John H. Bankhead, or either of them, is entitled to membership in the United States Senate " from Alabama.[39] A resolution in the following Congress declared Mr. Bankhead elected.[40] Similarly, a House resolution of the seventy-third Congress referred a controversy over a Louisiana election, Kemp versus Sanders, to the Committee on Elections # 3,[41] whose report resulted in a further resolution which held the election null and void and declared that a vacancy existed.[42]

Of slightly different tenor was a resolution authorizing the Committee on Elections # 2 of the House to inquire into the right to a seat of Francis H. Shoemaker of Minnesota.[43] Previously convicted of a felony, he had been sent to the penitentiary. The conviction, it was found, had been on a charge

[38] S. Res. 111, 71st Cong., 2d Sess., December 6, 1929.

[39] S. Res. 485, 71st Cong., 3d Sess., February 28, 1931. See also S. Res. 467, 71st Cong., 3d Sess., and S. Res. 139, 72d Cong., 1st Sess.

[40] S. Res. 199, 72d Cong., 1st Sess.

[41] H. Res. 202, 73d Cong., 2d Sess., January 3, 1934. In this instance, opposing groups in Louisiana had submitted to the House a certificate of election for each candidate. The resolution was " offered in accord with the wishes of the Louisiana delegation in Congress."

[42] H. Res. 231, 73d Cong., 2d Sess.

[43] H. Res. 6, 73d Cong., 1st Sess., March 10, 1933.

of sending defamatory statements through the mails; Shoemaker, receiving a letter addressed to " F. H. Shoemaker, editor Organized Farmer, any place in the world but Red Wing, Minnesota ", had returned the courtesy by replying to " R. W. Putnam, Robber of widows and orphans, Red Wing, Minnesota." The committee found no reason to deny Shoemaker his seat.[44]

INVESTIGATIONS MAY AID AS WELL AS CURB THE ADMINISTRATION. Several of the examples already cited sharpen the earlier assertion that a precise classification of inquiries is impossible. An investigation frequently resists an assignment to any one group, however flexibly it is defined. And further complicating any neat segregation is a welter of cross currents induced in many instances by considerations which are partisan or personal.

One of the more distinct underlying classifications can be drawn on the basis of the consequences of investigation to the Administration.[45] Leaving aside the membership inquiries, the bulk of investigations fall within either of two broad categories: those curbing [46] the Administration, and those aiding the Administration. Thus, most of the supervisory inquiries, aiming at discipline or at calling attention to maladministration, may be allotted to the former. A peak for investigations calculated to restrain an Administration was reached in the early twenties when such curbing was perhaps the primary feature of Congressional inquiry. At this time an attitude of " stand by " pervaded the Administration and a sense of defeatism marked the official minority. Conditions in the Senate, however, permitted the dissident Republicans, in combination

---

[44] Although the investigations of lobbying have been included under the " informing " heading, they would not be out of place in the " membership " group. Such inquiries offer pointed illustration of the difficulties of an absolute classification.

[45] See *supra*, p. 16, footnote, for the definition of "Administration."

[46] " Curbing ", as used in this study, also involves vigilance by Congress, which may or may not result in actual restraint.

with the Democrats, to constitute an intermittent majority for purposes, at least, of criticism. When malfeasance and misfeasance entered administration, apparently meeting no strong resistance from within, the check came from without, in the form of Congressional investigations. Because the more important studies of investigating were made during these days of Harding and Coolidge, it may be that the curbing aspect has been exaggerated. In comparatively rare instances have the inquiries of the past decade been motivated by any desire to uncover inefficiency or impropriety on the part of the executive branch. A few examples—in addition to the examination of the Bureau of Air Commerce,[47] the analysis by the Senate committee of the 1938 campaign expenditures,[48] and the joint inquiry into the Tennessee Valley Authority [49]—reflect their relative insignificance. Early in 1932 the Senate Committee on Agriculture and Forestry was asked to investigate the activities and operations of the Federal Farm Board.[50] This agency, created by the agricultural marketing act of 1929, had lost more than two-thirds of a $500,000,000 revolving fund which was appropriated for the stabilization of the prices of agricultural commodities. The report, issued in 1935 by a subcommittee guided by Senator McNary who in the meantime had found himself a member of the minority instead of the majority party, carried a sympathetic tone illustrated by the statement that the Farm Board " made its loans . . . without the benefit of the certainties which experience since has taught." [51]

[47] See *supra*, p. 25.

[48] See *supra*, p. 19.

[49] See *supra*, p. 28. Not until the ultimate effects of the TVA investigation are more clear cut, if ever, can it be arbitrarily classified as aiding or curbing the Administration. Both the opponents and the supporters of the Tennessee Valley project managed to find a degree of comfort from the hearings. See the committee's report, S. Doc. 56, 76th Cong., 1st Sess., April 3, 1939.

[50] S. Res. 42, 72d Cong., 1st Sess., April 11, 1932.

[51] S. Rept. 1456, 74th Cong., 1st Sess., August 23, 1935.

President Roosevelt's personal secretary, Louis M. Howe, also seemed a proper subject of investigation for his part in the purchase of toilet kits for the Civilian Conservation Corps,[52] but the investigating committee found no evidence of corruption or improper motive.[53]

The efforts of the committees of the House to uncover improprieties of the Administration were almost nil, even after January 1932 when President Hoover faced a House controlled by Democrats. The only two investigations which created any appreciable furore came during the Presidency of Mr. Roosevelt.[54] The first began in 1934 when the House Committee on Military Affairs inquired into alleged profiteering and maladministration in the War Department.[55] The committee, reporting a number of irregularities, recommended the removal of several executives in the Department including General Foulois, chief of the army air corps.[56] The second outstanding disparagement of the Administration by an inquiring committee of the House came in 1938 from the previously mentioned Dies investigation of un-American activities.[57] The

[52] S. Res. 88, 73d Cong., 1st Sess., June 2, 1933.

[53] S. Rept. 144, 73d Cong., 1st Sess., June 12, 1933.

[54] An investigation of the impeachment charges against Secretary of the Treasury Andrew Mellon in 1932 were discontinued when he was sent to London as an ambassador. See *supra*, p. 29, footnote.

[55] H. Res. 275, 73d Cong., 2d Sess., March 2, 1934.

[56] H. Repts. 1506, 2005, and 2060, 73d Cong.; and H. Repts. 3, 4, 1884, 2063, 2289, 2680, and 3010, 74th Cong. Even this investigation, voted immediately following the annulment of the government's airmail contracts with private companies and after several of the army planes which were used as substitutes had crashed, roused a suspicion that a part of its aim lay in removing any blame from the President's shoulders. The dismissal of General Foulois was recommended principally because he had procured supplies without competitive bidding, and also because he had told the Postmaster General he was "quite certain" that, in spite of only limited experience in night flying by many of the air corps pilots, the army could handle the mail. The Secretary of War, after an investigation, cleared but reprimanded General Foulois. Later, through a reorganization, the General lost some authority. The next year he resigned.

[57] See *supra*, p. 25.

intensity of the attacks from this source apparently was for the most part unforeseen. Had the Administration anticipated the line of march of the inquiry, it probably would have tried to block the scheme, although the chairman of the Rules Committee was sympathetic to the resolution.[58]

But, as already suggested, supervisory investigations are not necessarily assaults. They may, by ascertaining the needs of the executive departments, provide assistance to the Administration. Thus, the study of the avoidance of income taxes,[59] already treated, brought revisions in the tax laws desired by the Treasury Department. Another type of aid, essentially defensive, may be illustrated by the 1934 inquiry [60] following the charges by W. A. Wirt, an Indiana educator, of " reds " in the federal government. An open investigation of him and of some of those whom he accused served to minimize the charges.

The activities in connection with the inquiries in 1936 looking toward administrative reorganization form an interesting example of agile jockeying by the Executive in an effort to control the effect of an investigation. Rumor has it that President Roosevelt late in 1935 had before him for signature a letter suggesting an extra-governmental inquiry into the possibilities of better equipping the Executive for his managerial duties. Before he had signed it, however, the Senate passed a resolution introduced by Senator Byrd authorizing a select committee to investigate the executive agencies of the government with a view to coordination and economy.[61] The Presi-

[58] Although the Administration apparently hoped to block a continuation of the inquiry in the seventy-sixth Congress, any efforts along these lines were recognized to be futile. The investigation, by 1939, was supported by many Congressmen who interpreted the 1938 elections as indicating a reaction to the New Deal. Moreover, the committee was able to meet some of the criticism of its activities to date by arguing that the inquiry was far from completed. The investigation was continued by H. Res. 26 and H. Res. 81, 76th Cong., 1st Sess., February 3, 1939 and February 9, 1939.

[59] See *supra*, p. 26.

[60] H. Res. 317, 73d Cong., 2d Sess., March 29, 1934.

[61] S. Res. 217, 74th Cong., 2d Sess., February 24, 1936.

dent maneuvered skillfully to take over direction. On March 20 he wrote Speaker Byrns suggesting the creation of a House committee similar to the Senate's to " cooperate with me and the committee that I shall name in making this study . . . to avoid duplication of effort in the task of research." [62] Two days later he appointed a commission of three to study the problem from the point of view of over-all management. The House committee, set up by a resolution of April 29,[63] worked closely with the Senate committee in examining the individual agencies, although both committees entrusted the actual research to the Brookings Institution. It was perhaps inevitable that a number of conflicts appeared in the reports and recommendations of the President's committee and the committees of Congress. At any rate, the confusions generated by the disagreements on the part of the two groups of experts undoubtedly eased the task of the forces working for the defeat of the bills designed to effect the proposals of the President's committee.

It is seen, therefore, that the inquiries which have been classified as supervisory may aid as well as curb the Administration. But the other types of investigations likewise may either help or work against an Administration. Thus, the Hoover Administration was embarrassed when the Senate committee investigating stock exchanges and banking practices disclosed some of the conditions which had existed during the Republican ascendancy of the twenties.[64] An outstanding feature of the period covered by the present study, however, was the demonstration of the diversified possibilities of direct aid to an Administration by means of investigation. Because an Administration may be identified with a particular legislative program and because its prestige may to a large extent depend on its ability to have its proposals enacted into law, the inquiries which are designed to bring about this action may be

[62] *Congressional Record*, 74th Cong., 2d Sess., p. 4146, March 23, 1936.

[63] H. Res. 460, 74th Cong., 2d Sess., April 29, 1936.

[64] See *infra*, p. 40.

PURPOSES OF INVESTIGATIONS 39

of real assistance to an Administration. Experience under the New Deal — when, in direct contrast to the previous decade, a strong majority, Presidentially led, was committed to a program of social change — showed a development of this legislative-Administrative collaboration to a degree perhaps unprecedented.

Thus, an investigation was sometimes neatly arranged to reinforce a recommendation by the President regarding major legislation. The lobby inquiries of 1935,[65] for example, illustrated organized efforts by committees to arouse public opinion, and opened the way for the passage of laws restricting utility holding companies. A particularly clever tactical move was their timing to break at the moment when Congress was considering both the Wheeler Rayburn bill [66] to regulate utilities, and the amendments [67] broadening the scope of the Tennessee Valley Authority act. On July 1, 1935, the House defeated, by a vote of 216 to 146, the so-called " death sentence " clause of the Wheeler Rayburn bill which compelled the simplification of each electric utility holding company into one integrated system. A House resolution ordering an investigation of lobbying both for and against the bill was passed on July 8.[68] A Senate probe was ordered three days later. The testimony taken at the hearings, and well publicized throughout the nation, with reference to the methods and expenditures of the utility holding companies in attempting to defeat the bill, undoubtedly must be considered an important reason for the

[65] Res. 288, 74th Cong., 1st Sess., July 8, 1935; S. Res. 165, 74th Cong., 1st Sess., July 11, 1935.

[66] 49 Stat. 803.

[67] 49 Stat. 1075.

[68] The House committee, unlike the Senate committee, was interested in investigating the pressure from the proponents (including the Administration) as well as from the opponents of the bill. That the two committees were not exactly pulling together was suggested by their battle to obtain the testimony of H. C. Hopson. See the reports which were submitted by the committees on this incident, S. Rept. 1272, 74th Cong., 1st Sess., August 14, 1935, and H. Rept. 1803, 74th Cong., 1st Sess., August 15, 1935.

approval by the House on August 22 of the "death sentence" in only a slightly modified form.[69] For instance, the chairman of the Senate committee inserted in the record of the hearings on August 16 a summary based on sworn statements from the managers of telegraph offices in twenty towns showing that of 31,580 telegrams sent to Washington on the Wheeler bill all but thirteen were filed and paid for by representatives of the utility companies.[70] Moreover, on August 14, after more than three weeks of futile search for H. C. Hopson of the Associated Gas and Electric system, and after he had declined to accept a summons on the thirteenth, the committee unanimously recommended that the Senate should arrest both Hopson and his lawyer "and cause them to be brought before the bar of this Senate . . . to show cause, if any they have, why they should not be punished for contempt of this Senate." [71] These and other activities by the committee also helped to insure the enactment of the T. V. A. amendments which were signed by the President on the last day of the month.

Similarly helpful to the Roosevelt Administration was the investigation into stock exchange practices and banking.[72] Begun rather inconspicuously in 1932, it was in some quarters termed a "whitewash" proposition. But upon the employment of Ferdinand Pecora as chief counsel in 1933, not long before the change in the Administration, the inquiry spectacularly called the nation's attention to the questionable practices of certain "money changers" and made easier the task of enacting such Roosevelt-supported legislation as the banking acts of 1933 [73]

[69] The approval came with the adoption of a resolution, 219 to 142, instructing the House conferees to recede and concur in a compromise proposed by the Senate. The compromise permitted the existence of holding companies to the second degree and allowed other less important exceptions to the requirement for simplification.

[70] Hearings, p. 1014.

[71] S. Rept. 1272, 74th Cong., 1st Sess. The Senate did not order the arrest, however, since Mr. Hopson appeared before the committee on August 15.

[72] S. Res. 84, 72d Cong., 1st Sess., March 4, 1932.

[73] 48 Stat. 162.

and 1935,[74] the securities act of 1933 [75] and the securities exchange act of 1934.[76] The opposition to the passage of the securities exchange act, for instance, was pronounced. There was a decided reaction to the original securities act during 1933 and 1934. Business complained vigorously of the new chains. At the same time, however, the committee's exposures contributed to the resignation of the chairman of the National City Bank of New York, to the discontinuance of the Chase National Bank's life pension of $100,000 annually for the ex-chairman of the board, and, at least in part, to the attempted suicide of the founder of the Harriman National Bank and Trust Company. The securities exchange act of 1934 therefore became an advance rather than a retreat and extended the regulation to stock exchanges.

Less subtle assistance was given to the Administration at the direct request of the Executive. The investigation of " monopoly ", although it was not conducted by the exact type of committee suggested, will serve as an example of an inquiry voted in response to the expressed wish of the President. A message from Mr. Roosevelt to Congress on April 29, 1938 called for " a thorough study of the concentration of economic power in American industry and the effect of that concentration upon the decline of competition," and proposed an appropriation of $500,000 for its conduct by the Federal Trade Commission, the Department of Justice, the Securities and Exchange Commission, " and such other agencies of the government as have special experience in various phases of the inquiry." [77] The current atmosphere was favorable to such a study, provided it be orderly. From the standpoint of both the government and business a better defined official attitude toward monopoly was desirable. Since the birth of the National Recovery Administration five years before, and even after the

[74] 49 Stat. 684.
[75] 48 Stat. 74.
[76] 48 Stat. 881.
[77] S. Doc. 173, 75th Cong., 3d Sess.

Schechter case, the Administration had wavered between
" trust busting " and a greater toleration of business combinations.[78] Moreover, no broad governmental study of the problem had been made since the hearings by the committees of
both houses on the anti-trust legislation of 1914.[79] Congress
was not willing, however, to allow the investigation to be conducted only by administrators. A joint resolution introduced
by Senator O'Mahoney provided for an inquiry by a committee of three Senators, three members of the House, and five
representatives of the administrative departments and agencies.[80] Of the $500,000 appropriation, $100,000 was to be available to the committee and $400,000 " as the President shall
direct, among the departments and agencies represented on the
committee." One of several amendments suggested by the
Committee on the Judiciary would have retained for the committeemen a closer control of the funds: " $400,000 shall be
available, on application by the committee for allocation by the
President among the departments and agencies." [81] But the
Administration leaders, successfully defeating the proviso,
28 yeas to 40 nays, restored the $400,000 to Presidential dis-
cretion. Congress's clear majority on the committee was lost
by the enlargement of the group to twelve members—six Congressmen and six representatives of the departments and agen-

[78] Section 5 of Title I of the NIRA provided: "any code, agreement, or
license, approved, prescribed, or issued and in effect under this title, and any
action complying with the provisions thereof . . . shall be exempt from the
provisions of the anti-trust laws of the United States." That the anti-trust
laws were not to be completely relaxed was indicated, however, by the
stipulation in section 3 that the President might approve the codes of fair
competition if they were "not designed to promote monopolies."

[79] Hearings before the Committee on the Judiciary, House of Representatives, 63d Cong., 2d Sess., on *Trust Legislation,* 35 parts (beginning Dec. 9,
1913); also, Hearings before the Committee on Interstate Commerce,
U. S. Senate, 63d Cong., 2d Sess., on *Bills Relating to Trust Legislation,*
2 volumes (beginning Feb. 26, 1914). An important study of the same general
subject was made by the U. S. Industrial Commission of 1898 (30 Stat. 476).

[80] 52 Stat. 705, June 16, 1938.

[81] *Congressional Record,* 75th Cong., 3d Sess., p. 8502, June 8, 1938.

cies; the committee, however, elected Senator O'Mahoney to the important post of chairman, and chose Representative Sumners as vice-chairman.[82]

Cooperation between an investigating committee and the Administration may also lie in the assistance that a Congressional inquiry can give to an executive body whose activities are closely articulated with Presidential policy. This indirection may be thought necessary because of doubts as to whether the investigative powers of administrative bodies are equal to those of legislative committees.[83] Thus, the Senate Committee on Interstate Commerce conducted an inquiry into the financing of railroads [84] partly for the purpose of acquiring information which the Interstate Commerce Commission felt it could not obtain.[85]

An investigating committee may collaborate with an Administration in still other ways. For example, a reflection on another Administration, with the implication that the current management is more honest or efficient, may benefit the latter. Two or three inquiries by the Senate and House into alleged maladministration by the previous régime were sponsored after the change of control in 1933. The chief among these was the Senate inquiry into the air mail and ocean mail contracts.[86] The resolution, passed on February 25, 1932, authorized the selection of a committee of five composed of three members of the majority party and two of the minority, but stipulated that the appointments should not be made until after March 4 when the majority would change. The revelations by the committee of the procedure by which the contracts were granted had the effect of discrediting the former Administration to some degree, although the later repercussions which followed

[82] See *infra*, p. 146.

[83] See Chapter VI for a discussion of the differences.

[84] S. Res. 71, 74th Cong., 1st Sess., May 20, 1935.

[85] See *infra*, p. 153.

[86] S. Res. 349, 72d Cong., 2d Sess., February 25, 1933.

the army's unsuccessful flying of the mail [87] perhaps over-balanced the advantages to the party in power. Again, a resolution in April 1933 requested an inquiry by the Senate Committee on the Judiciary into the alleged laxness on the part of the Department of Justice during President Hoover's term in investigating violations of the law in the Harriman National Bank.[88]

In an election year an investigation may supply handy campaign ammunition for the party in power. Thus, the Senate committee inquiring into lobbying devoted a portion of its. public hearings in 1936 to such organizations as the Crusaders, the Farmers' Independence Council, and the Sentinels of the Republic, and revealed that several of these groups, hostile to President Roosevelt and the New Deal, received funds from the same individuals, some of whom were wealthy industrialists and financiers. During the same campaign of 1936, the Senate Committee on Campaign Expenditures [89] lent assistance to the Administration by disclosing, on the eve of a speech in Maine by Alfred M. Landon, the Republican Presidential candidate, that some of the backers of the conservative American Liberty League had contributed to the Republican campaign fund in Maine.

The utilization of investigations as tools of the Administration became an issue of sufficient import to elicit a protest from Mr. Landon: " No legal hairsplitting can hide the difference between an investigating committee that is trying to get information useful in the framing of laws and an investigating committee that is indulging in a fishing expedition into the private affairs of private citizens—a committee that is out to get the crooks and a committee that is out to get the critics. In the last three and a half years, Congressional investigations have budded and blossomed in unusually rank profusion. No

[87] See *infra*, p. 89.

[88] S. Res. 55, 73d Cong., 1st Sess., April 18, 1933.

[89] S. Res. 225, 74th Cong., 2d Sess., April 1, 1936.

soil of real or fancied wrongdoing is so poor it will not sprout a full-fledged investigation." [90]

PERSONAL MOTIVES FOR INVESTIGATIONS.   An analysis of the purposes of investigations leads to a consideration of the personal factors which are involved. The benefits accruing to individual legislators as a consequence of inquiries have been incessantly featured in popular articles on the subject. The net result probably is an over-emphasis in the public mind of this phase. Nevertheless, a not insignificant incentive to an investigation may lie in the personal profit anticipated by a member of Congress. The gain may consist in nothing more than enviable publicity. Many inquiries make newspaper copy. Many reputations, for better or worse, thus burgeon. Such names as Pujo, Walsh, Caraway, Black, or Nye doubtless would, in the absence of investigations, have been less familiar. The conclusion appears incontestable that investigations were a springboard which placed Senator Walsh in line for the office of Attorney General in 1933.[91] Indeed, the question may be raised whether Senator Black would have gone to the Supreme Court bench if he had never participated in investigations. True, considerable labor and grief may be involved in an inquiry. Senator Nye has emphasized the hardships and has maintained: " I have yet to meet the Member of Congress who has enjoyed the tremendous responsibility accompanying appointment to such a committee." [92] And in fairness to him, it should be added that intense pressure was necessary to win his consent to handle the investigation of the munitions industry. But Congressmen hardly can overlook these invitations to a position on the front page. Especially may this apply during Congressional recesses, when the members may have greater difficulty in gaining the headlines.

[90] *New York Times*, October 21, 1936, reporting his Los Angeles speech on the previous day.

[91] He was appointed on February 28, 1933, but died two days later.

[92] *Congressional Record*, 73d Cong., 1st Sess., p. 4182, May 25, 1933.

An investigation may also spring from the efforts of a member of Congress to win popularity. The good will sought may be of a general nature. Thus, in periods of rising prices a popular subject of inquiry has been the high prices of such staples as bread, sugar, and meat. More frequently an inquiry may be suggested with the object of favoring, and thereby gaining the endorsement of, a member's constituents. Most of the proposals of a local nature die in committee, but there are exceptions. The Senate, for instance, approved a resolution introduced by Senator Moore of New Jersey authorizing a grant of one thousand dollars to a select committee of three to study the claims against the United States Housing Authority by the City of New Brunswick, New Jersey.[93] A second example of an inquiry into a local subject was a study sponsored by Representative Beiter during the seventy-fourth Congress. Following the 1935 floods in his constituency in central New York, the authority of the House was obtained for an investigation into the conditions of the waterways in that section [94] and a committee appointed. But a companion resolution providing the expenses for the project failed to receive the approval of the Committee on Accounts.[95] Mr. Beiter and other members of the committee, therefore, agreed to pay their own expenses, and a report, recommending more federal relief, was submitted after a personal tour of inspection of the area affected.[96] Senator Pittman's activities with respect to silver may also be cited. Reference has already been made to his special committee on the administration of the silver purchase act.[97] A further investigatory result of his dominant attention to silver was his resolution authorizing an inquiry into the trade between the United States and China.[98] The hearings showed what the text

[93] S. Res. 165, 75th Cong., 1st Sess., August 14, 1937.

[94] H. Res. 298, 74th Cong., 1st Sess., July 18, 1935.

[95] H. Res. 299, 74th Cong., 1st Sess.

[96] *Congressional Record*, 74th Cong., 1st Sess., p. 12042, July 29, 1935.

[97] See *supra*, p. 27.

[98] S. Res. 256, 71st Cong., 2d Sess., June 2, 1930.

of the resolution had not, that the investigation was in the interests of silver, since Senator Pittman endeavored to show a relationship between the price of silver and the quantity of exports from the United States.[99]

A further stimulus to inquiry is bound up in the pet hobbies or hates of individual Congressmen, although these in turn may be motivated in part by the efforts to please constituents. One case in point involves Senator Ellison D. Smith and the alleged abuses in the cotton markets. Following a long service in the upper house, the South Carolina Senator became in 1933 the chairman of the Committee on Agriculture and Forestry. His unwavering solicitude for his home state's principal crop has earned him the title of " Cotton Ed." Within the last dozen years he has sponsored or been closely associated with three investigations probing suspected manipulations of the cotton market. Asking in 1928 for an investigation of " the decline in the price of cotton," [100] Senator Smith was selected to head an inquiring subcommittee of five from the Committee on Agriculture and Forestry. One year and a half later a new resolution sought to throw light on the alleged manipulations on the New York, New Orleans, and Chicago cotton exchanges.[101] Although the investigation was instigated this time by Senator Heflin, Senator Smith was chosen as a member of the committee and actively participated in the interrogation of the witnesses. The seventy-fourth Congress brought the third probe following a rapid decline in the prices of cotton on March 11, 1935.[102] As the sponsor of the resolution, and now chairman of the Committee on Agriculture and Forestry, Senator Smith again directed the inquiry.[103]

[99] James A. Perkins, *Congress Investigates Our Foreign Relations* (unpublished dissertation, Princeton, 1937), p. 107.

[100] S. Res. 142, 70th Cong., 1st Sess., February 15, 1928.

[101] S. Res. 152, 71st Cong., 1st Sess., November 14, 1929.

[102] S. Res. 103, 74th Cong., 1st Sess., March 16, 1935.

[103] Senator Smith also seems to have developed an antipathy in William L. Clayton, an important cotton merchant. In each of these three inquiries, Mr. Clayton was a chief suspect and was rigorously examined by the Senator.

At times, however, these hobbies or hates are only remotely motivated, if at all, by a wish to cater to constituents or by a desire for publicity. It must be borne in mind that a legislator sometimes may, with little or no consideration for any personal gain, battle for a " cause ". Thus, it may be argued that Representative Dickstein's constant annoyance at " un-American " activities in the United States is in the nature of an obsession which is scarcely stimulated by political expedience. Introducing a resolution in the House in 1934 to investigate Nazi and other propaganda activities originating in foreign countries,[104] he declined, because of Jewish blood, to act as the chairman, but accepted a post on the committee which submitted a report early in 1935. The next year, when the " Black Legion " gained nationwide prominence, he sponsored two House resolutions and one concurrent resolution seeking to probe this together with other " un-American " groups. All three were pigeon-holed in the Rules Committee. By a renewed effort he brought a resolution of the same type [105] to the floor of the following Congress, but a wave of non-partisan opposition deluged it under a tabling vote of 184 to 38.[106] The next move by Representative Dickstein was to support a newly suggested inquiry into " un-American " activities embodied in a resolution introduced by Representative Dies.[107] The approval of the House was obtained, but Mr. Dickstein, reported " angry ", was not made a member of the committee of seven.

SUMMARY.   Both houses of Congress, in the performance of each of their major responsibilities, employ Congressional investigations. A convenient classification of these inquiries may, therefore, be based on the legislative function which is being discharged. Thus, investigations may assist Congress to legislate, to supervise the executive, to inform the public, and

[104] H. Res. 198, 73d Cong., 2d Sess., March 20, 1934.
[105] H. Res. 88, 75th Cong., 1st Sess.
[106] *Congressional Record*, 75th Cong., 1st Sess., p. 3290, April 8, 1937.
[107] H. Res. 282, 75th Cong., 3d Sess., May 26, 1938.

to perform its "membership" duties. Most inquiries, however, serve more than one of these purposes. It is impracticable, therefore, to attempt a rigid segregation of all investigations into the four categories suggested. Moreover, the underlying purposes of investigations complicate any precise classification. An inquiry may, for example, be principally motivated by personal considerations. And one of the outstanding investigatorial developments since 1933 has been the demonstration of the extent to which Congressional inquiries may become useful tools of an Administration.

CHAPTER III

PROCEDURE

BOTH the immediate and ultimate aims of inquiries are widely diversified. The objectives of the investigators go far toward determining the values finally derived. But good intentions are not enough. Regardless of the ends sought, the procedure usually remains a fundamental determinant of an investigation's general success or failure. Careless procedure may nullify noble purpose.

Because the procedure is controlled by the personnel of a committee, consideration must be given to the appointing power. Courtesy in both houses suggests that the sponsor of an inquiry should become the chairman of the investigating group. When the inquiry is made by a standing committee, this generally means the appointment, by the chairman, of a subcommittee headed and steered by the introducer of the resolution.[1] Likewise, the choice for the chairmanship of a select committee is normally a foregone conclusion. The other members usually are chosen following consultations between the Vice-President or Speaker and the Majority and Minority Leaders. Occasionally, however, the appointing officer may fail to confer with the leaders. The selection of the joint committee for inquiring into the Tennessee Valley Authority apparently provides an example of Vice-Presidential refusal to be shackled by the consultative custom. Prior to the enactment of the resolution,[2] heated debate centered on the merits and demerits of the Authority and its work. Senator Bridges, the sponsor

1 Only rarely does a Senator or Representative sponsor an investigation by a standing committee to which he does not belong. An exception was Senator Hiram Johnson's resolution directing an investigation by the Finance Committee of the sales of foreign securities in the United States (S. Res. 19, 72d Cong., 1st Sess., December 10, 1931). Although not a member of the committee, Senator Johnson participated in the hearings. Investigating committees, on occasion, invite interested members of Congress to attend hearings.

2 52 Stat. 154, April 4, 1938.

of another resolution directing an investigation of the same subject, was especially vociferous in his condemnation. But Mr. Garner, seemingly intent on an inquiry as calm as possible, angered the New Hampshire Senator by passing over the members known to be strongly sympathetic or opposed to the project, and appointing those believed to be more impartial. The veracity of the reports that the Vice-President had not consulted the leaders before choosing the committee was suggested by three refusals to serve.

IMPORTANCE OF PREPARATION PRIOR TO HEARINGS. It may be that disproportionate attention has been given in the past to the more dramatic part of investigations, the hearings, and that due respect has not been paid to the less spectacular prehearings stage. It is during this period of gestation, following the passage of a Senate or House resolution of authorization, that especial care must be taken to insure an effective investigation.

RESOLUTIONS ARE SOMETIMES UNHEEDED. It should be noted that the committees occasionally disregard resolutions. But the examples are insignificant. Inasmuch as an inquiry is generally turned over to the committee or individual suggesting it, a decision not to investigate usually provokes no questions. So far as the writer is aware, no case has been presented in the past decade of a deliberate effort to shelve a subject by inaction. A House resolution [3] authorized the Committee on the Civil Service to determine whether each state had its quota of federal employees in accordance with the civil service act. The clerk of the committee, in answer to a request for the results of the investigation, wrote: " Honorable Lamar Jeffers, of Alabama, was Chairman of this Committee when the resolution . . . was passed. . . . As I recall, Mr. Jeffers appointed a subcommittee, with himself as Chairman, to conduct this investigation. I believe they had one or two informal discussions with some of the officials of the Civil Service Com-

[3] H. Res. 146, 73d Cong., 1st Sess., June 1, 1933.

mission, but never actually proceeded with the investigation. Soon after that, Mr. Jeffers was engaged in a heated political campaign in his district in Alabama, was defeated for renomination in the Democratic Primary, and this matter died out from lack of interest." [4] Also to be noted was the absence of any activity pursuant to a resolution sponsored by the Senate Committee on Banking and Currency which authorized it to " investigate from time to time operations . . . and the procedure" of the Reconstruction Finance Corporation, and provided that " the committee shall report from time to time to the Senate the results of its investigations." [5] The committee, according to its chairman, Duncan U. Fletcher, did not deem an investigation necessary: " Frankly, members of the Committee had no particular activity of the Reconstruction Finance Corporation in mind when they asked for an extension of the power incorporated in Senate Resolution 69. It was merely a precautionary step. Moreover, the resolution contained no mandatory provision for either an investigation or report to be made to the Senate." [6]

But, assuming that steps are taken toward an inquiry, three major tasks immediately present themselves to the investigatory body: (1) determining the extent of the investigation,

---

[4] Letter of March 11, 1936.

[5] S. Res. 69, 73d Cong., 1st Sess., May 4, 1933.

[6] Letter of March 13, 1936. Both of these resolutions " authorized" the investigations, as distinct from the more common " authorize and direct." That resolutions are sometimes sponsored with no clear goal in view is illustrated by one other example. Early in 1934 the Senate Committee on Commerce asked, and received by unanimous consent without any explanation or debate, approval for a resolution providing: " That the Committee on Commerce or a subcommittee thereof give study to the merchant marine and aeronautic services with a view to the preservation and promotion of the commerce and trade of the United States " (S. Res. 183, 73d Cong., 2d Sess., February 20, 1934). No money or compelling power were conferred. The chairman of the committee, interrogated concerning the activities resulting from the resolution, pointed to the hearings, begun two years later, on three Senate bills designed to develop a strong merchant marine (Hearings on S. 3500, S. 4110, S. 4111, beginning March 9, 1936). These hearings, however, could have been conducted without the resolution.

(2) choosing and organizing a staff, and (3) determining the most effective means of obtaining the desired information.

DEFINING THE SCOPE OF THE INVESTIGATION. The extent of the investigation, of course, is limited by the resolution of authorization. A distinct restriction on the activities of investigating committees is the not uncommon stipulation that the hearings shall be conducted only in the District of Columbia. A stock criticism of investigations has been that too often their chief accomplishment lies in providing opportunities for Congressional pleasure jaunts. Charges of this sort were hurled, for instance, at a Senate committee on campaign expenditures, headed by Senator Nye, which held hearings in a number of states.[7] The defenders of wide traveling by committees, however, have by no means been lacking. Any impartial judgment on the subject should take into account the possible economy involved in transporting a small group of investigators rather than a host of witnesses. But both the Senate and House, aware of the possible and sometimes actual abuses, have recently tended to keep the inquiries within the bounds of the capital.

In the main, however, a resolution is drawn to provide a committee with as broad powers as it may conceivably need. Because he who drafts a resolution frequently becomes the chairman of the investigating committee, the tendency is to impose few restraints. Thus, Senator Brookhart, in the debate on the authorization of an inquiry into lobbying,[8] addressed Senator Caraway: "I desire to ask the Senator from Arkansas whether the resolution is broad enough to cover investigation of the social lobby." The future chairman's reply was significant: " Yes, sir; it is broad enough to investigate anything in which one might feel interested." A similar attitude was expressed by Representative Greenwood, the chairman of a subcommittee of the Rules Committee which had favorably re-

[7] S. Res. 215, 71st Cong., 2d Sess., April 10, 1930.
[8] S. Res. 20, 71st Cong., 1st Sess., October 1, 1929.

ported a resolution directing an investigation into " un-American " activities in the United States.[9] Asked for a definition
of terms in what seemed to some Representatives an all-inclu-
sive mandate, he added to the uncertainty by exclaiming: " I
do not expect to be a member of that committee. The committee may read this resolution and put whatever interpretation they see fit upon it without any limitation, so far as I am
concerned." Further illustrative of broad phrasing was a final
clause added to the powers conferred on another committee on
lobbying to investigate " any other matter or proposal affecting
legislation." [10] Such blank checks are far from desirable. The
self-restraints of the investigators should not be wholly relied
upon to keep them within the bounds of propriety. A barrier
should be erected at some point.

The difficulties involved in establishing the proper bounds by
means of a resolution immediately become evident, however.
The limits should not be drawn too narrowly. The slightest
loophole left in a resolution is almost certain to be found by
those who are being investigated. A select committee of the
House, for example, was granted authority [11] ostensibly sufficient for inquiring into the American Retail Federation, an
organization allegedly formed in the interests of such large-
scale retailers as department stores and chain stores. But six
weeks later, after information was refused to the committee,
Representative Patman appealed for the enactment of a new
resolution [12] because " When we started our investigation a
few days ago we discovered that this super lobby . . . (had)
changed their name." By the addition of the authority " to
investigate the trade practices of individuals, partnerships, and
corporations engaged in big-scale buying and selling of articles
at wholesale or retail," the inquiry was enabled to proceed as
originally contemplated.

[9] H. Res. 88, 75th Cong., 1st Sess., not approved.
[10] S. Res. 165, 74th Cong., 1st Sess., July 11, 1935.
[11] H. Res. 203, 74th Cong., 1st Sess., April 24, 1935.
[12] H. Res. 239, 74th Cong., 1st Sess., June 4, 1935.

Extraordinary care is demanded therefore in the drafting of the resolutions directing investigations. This is not to say that the course of an inquiry can be completely charted before embarkation. A broadening of the activities of a committee may be discovered advisable only after an investigation has begun. Thus, the Senate Banking and Currency Committee probing stock exchange practices [13] found its steps leading so far into other financial fields that, impelled by the collapse of the country's banking system, it obtained approval for a supplementary inquiry into banking.[14] Such an expansion of authority may in this case have been fully justified. But the tardy grants of power to other investigating committees may point to carelessly-drawn terms of reference. For example, a Senate committee was instructed to investigate " the rapid decline of the price of cotton on the cotton exchanges on or about March 11, 1935." [15] Less than two months later, a second resolution was found necessary to enlarge the scope to include the " activities (of agencies and persons) connected with the cotton business." [16] And by another three months a further grant of authority was added giving the committee power to inquire into the " causes of the decline (in the price of cotton) . . . on, prior, and subsequent to March 11, 1935." [17] Had the original resolution been more carefully drafted, both Congress and the committee might have been saved the time consumed in the formalities necessary for the adoption of the two additional resolutions.

Appropriations may also act as an important restraint on an investigation. The resolutions authorizing inquiries by committees which require funds must run the gauntlet of two standing committees. The customary procedure in the House calls for one resolution reported by the Committee on Rules to

[13] S. Res. 84, 72d Cong., 1st Sess., March 4, 1932.
[14] S. Res. 56, 73d Cong., 1st Sess., April 4, 1933.
[15] S. Res. 103, 74th Cong., 1st Sess., March 16, 1935.
[16] S. Res. 125, 74th Cong., 1st Sess., May 7, 1935.
[17] S. Res. 172, 74th Cong., 1st Sess., July 30, 1935.

authorize the investigation, and a second by the Committee on Accounts to grant the appropriation. The Senate generally passes only one resolution which has been referred to two committees including the Committee to Audit and Control the Contingent Expenses of the Senate. The downward revision of appropriations by the latter committee has tended to become so habitual that the sympathizers with various investigations currently decry the " conservatism " of the committee.[18] To reinforce this contention they point to the comparative ease with which, for instance, the Federal Communications Commission obtained, without the necessity of approval by the Contingent Expenses committee, a total of $1,500,000 to investigate the American Telephone and Telegraph and other telephone companies; while the Senate Committee on Interstate Commerce, for the purpose of inquiring into the nation's railroads, received, after considerable effort, three allotments totalling $250,000.[19]

Once launched, however, an inquiry is rarely left in midstream. Investigators frequently may undertake a project larger in scale than warranted by the original grant of funds, with a reasonable assurance that the material to be unearthed will convince the Senate or House of a need for further appropriations. The net result in many instances, therefore, is a seeming reluctance to estimate the probable total expenditures. A demonstration of vagueness, extreme but nevertheless symbolic, comes from an earlier Congress. The debate was centered on a resolution,[20] offered by Representative Lloyd, to grant additional funds for a current investigation of the steel trust. In

[18] The present members are Senators Byrnes, Tydings, Truman, and Townsend. Senators Byrnes, Tydings, and Townsend have served on the committee since 1933 or before. Senator Truman was appointed on January 10, 1939.

[19] The Communications Commission received three allotments: 49 Stat. 45; 49 Stat. 1601; and 50 Stat. 11. The Interstate Commerce Committee's three appropriations were contained in S. Res. 71, 74th Cong., 1st Sess.; S. Res. 227, 74th Cong., 2d Sess.; and S. Res. 86, 75th Cong., 1st Sess.

[20] H. Res. 469, 62d Cong., 2d Sess., April 11, 1912.

reply to Representative Mann's query, " Mr. Speaker, can the gentleman tell us whether this will be the last installment of this continued story," Mr. Lloyd ventured: " Mr. Speaker, I can not answer except to say this, that unless it is necessary to ask for an additional appropriation or allowance it will be sufficient." Mr. Mann's only comment was: "That is certainly a clear and frank statement." [21] That the original appropriation is no criterion of the total finally to be allotted to a committee is also illustrated by the inquiry into real estate bondholders' reorganizations.[22] Representative Sabath, the chief sponsor, went on record as follows:

Mr. Blanton. How much is going to be spent on this resolution?
Mr. Sabath. I really do not know. It would not be a large sum.

.   .   .   .

Mr. Blanton. Can the gentleman give me some idea of how much the gentleman intends to ask for?
Mr. Sabath. I cannot.
Mr. Blanton. Can the gentleman from New York (Mr. O'Connor), who knows something about it, tell us what he thinks this will cost? . . . How much is it intended to ask for under this resolution?
Mr. O'Connor. I will be frank gentlemen; I think at least $25,000.
Mr. Blanton. That sum is out of all reason.
Mr. Sabath. It will not cost that much.[23]

The first appropriation was $15,000 but it grew to $117,135. Other examples sharpen the point. The $5,000 given to the select committee of the Senate to investigate the ocean and air mail contracts,[24] for instance, was scarcely indicative of the total of $55,000 finally granted to it. The Senate munitions committee,[25] although it asked for $50,000, began its investi-

---

21 *Congressional Record*, 62d Cong., 2d Sess., p. 4618, April 11, 1912.
22 H. Res. 412, 73d Cong., 2d Sess., June 15, 1934.
23 *Congressional Record*, 73d Cong., 2d Sess., p. 11764, June 15, 1934.
24 S. Res. 349, 72d Cong., 2d Sess., February 25, 1933.
25 S. Res. 206, 73d Cong., 2d Sess., April 12, 1934.

gation with a $15,000 pittance which rose eventually to $133,-124 and might have continued to expand had not the chairman drawn vituperations on himself by casting reflections on former President Wilson.[26] The House Judiciary Committee's inquiry into the proceedings in bankruptcies [27] supplies one more illustration of a larger expenditure of funds than was predicted. The House of Representatives voted $5,000 to the committee, guided by Mr. Blanton's statement that the "resolution . . . is a proper resolution, properly framed, properly safeguarded, under which there will not be spent over $5,000, because I have the assurance of my good colleague from Texas, in whom we have all confidence, Mr. Sumners, chairman of the Judiciary Committee, who assures me that he is going to handle this investigation himself, and he does not believe there will be half of the $5,000 expended and guarantees that they will not expend over $5,000." [28] But in the next session, two additional allotments, totalling $12,500, were approved.[29]

The observation appears justified that resolutions directing inquiries are frequently drafted carelessly and with only hazy objectives in mind. This very vagueness makes further planning at some later stage essential. But even the most exact resolution will necessarily allow some discretion as to the scope of action. It therefore behooves a committee first to stake out its field of operations. Early attention to this delimiting is ordinarily indispensable to subsequent orderliness of procedure as well as to a full utilization of both time and money. The failure of some committees to map clearly-defined zones for action has invited investigations tending to ramble.

---

[26] The committee also was bitterly criticized in the Senate for its use of workers on relief in New York City. Senator Nye admitted the expenditure of $58,000 from relief funds for the committee. *Congressional Record*, 74th Cong., 2d Sess., p. 569, January 17, 1936.

[27] H. Res. 145, 73d Cong., 1st Sess., June 12, 1933.

[28] *Congressional Record*, 73d Cong., 1st Sess., p. 5791, June 12, 1933.

[29] H. Res. 228 and H. Res. 443, 73d Cong., 2d Sess.

SELECTING A STAFF. The second problem which an investigating committee must encounter is that of selecting a staff and organizing it for action. More often than not an investigation will be the offspring of some individual, sometimes to such an extent that it may be deemed a personal thing. Thus, the inquiry into infringements of civil liberties [30] was not inaccurately referred to as Senator LaFollette's investigation. To an equal degree the study of real estate bondholders' reorganization committees [31] was built around an individual, Representative Sabath. Likewise, we tend to think of the investigation of the munitions industry [32] as Senator Nye's. There is some evidence that the prestige of a Senator (ignoring for a moment the investigations in the House) adds a certain tone to an inquiry in which he actively participates, but the responsibilities adhering to the efficient management of an investigation are considerable. Someone must assume the role of field marshal. Before the hearings, long hours must be spent over the material collected by subordinates. During the hearings, nights should be given to planning carefully the next day's proceedings; extemporaneous and random questioning, although often relied upon, is not enough. Later, all the evidence must be digested and conclusions drawn. Such tasks, tremendous as they are, can be, and frequently are, handled by legislators. Senator LaFollette, for instance, was the keystone of his inquiry; studying the information gathered by his staff, he generally was the chief interrogator in the hearings.[33] But other less expert or less industrious probers have been guilty of handicapping fumbles. In recent years, therefore, there has developed an increased tendency for Congressmen to yield the general, or at least a partial, direction of the proceedings to

[30] S. Res. 266, 74th Cong., 2d Sess., June 6, 1936.

[31] H. Res. 412, 73d Cong., 2d Sess., June 15, 1934.

[32] S. Res. 206, 73d Cong., 2d Sess., April 12, 1934.

[33] He was frequently assisted by the other half of the committee of two, Senator Elbert Thomas. A few of the hearings were conducted by the members of the staff.

outsiders. For example, the Senate's Committee on Interstate Commerce, which was asked in 1930 to investigate the consolidation of railroad properties,[34] did no actual probing of its own, but depended on the study of an expert, and introduced a bill [35] based on the facts presented by him. And Senator Fletcher, chairman of the probe into stock exchanges and banking, assumed a backstage position, while Ferdinand Pecora became the chief inquisitor.[36] These positions were somewhat reversed in the munitions inquiry, where Senator Nye held the key role, although Stephen Raushenbush, the counsel to the committee, remained close to the center of the stage and formed an indispensable coordinator. Whether a Congressman or an outsider, however, it is generally this axial individual who selects the greater part of the staff.

One obstacle to acquiring a capable staff has been a provision in the recent bills appropriating funds for the expenses of special and select investigating committees that " no person shall be employed under this appropriation at a rate of compensation in excess of $3,600 per annum." [37] Among others, Senator Black called attention to this handicap: " It is because of this limitation on fees that committees are often compelled to get along without counsel, in which case the great burden of examining witnesses falls upon Senators and Congressmen who are members of the committee." [38] Not only for the interrogation but also for the field work, trained men are needed. Lawyers and accountants are especially demanded.[39]

[34] S. Res. 290, 71st Cong., 2d Sess., June 16, 1930.

[35] S. 6276, 71st Cong.

[36] A close association was maintained, however, between the chairman and the counsel.

[37] The Senate began establishing this limit in the seventy-second Congress; the House followed suit in the seventy-third, when practically all investigating committees were so restricted.

[38] " Inside a Senate Investigation," 172 *Harpers Magazine* 275 (1936).

[39] The type of staff which is required varies according to the nature of the inquiry. Moreover, the requirements for a particular investigation may change as the investigation progresses. Robert Wohlforth, the secretary of the com-

Public-spirited citizens sometimes have made tremendous financial sacrifices to serve committees. Mr. Pecora, employed under this limitation, also was subject to the fifteen percent economy cut of 1933 and thereby received only $255 a month. An interesting exemption from the limitation was made when the Senate committee on lobbying came in conflict with William Randolph Hearst in the courts.[40] The publisher, denied an in-

mittee investigating the infringements of civil liberties (S. Res. 266, 74th Cong., 2d Sess.), attests to the necessity for variations in the types of the staffs, but nevertheless suggests that " Roughly, a staff to get an inquiry under way would need (on the basis of ten) three attorneys, one research-economist, one accountant-statistician, one executive, four investigators plus clerical and stenographic personnel. It could be expanded on that basis depending upon the type and need of the inquiry." (Letter of March 8, 1939 to the writer.)

The Senate committee investigating the munitions industry (S. Res. 206, 73d Cong., 2d Sess.), for example, had, at various times, a total staff of fourteen persons. This figure does not include the committee's counsel, Stephen Raushenbush, the clerks and stenographers, or the persons who were borrowed from the relief rolls in New York City (see *supra*, p. 58, footnote). Of the fourteen, three were lawyers and two were accountants; the balance was composed of a specialist in international law, a financial writer, two free-lance newspaper men, and five persons who were doing, or had done, graduate work in the social sciences (three economists, one psychologist, and one political scientist).

The Senate Committee on Interstate Commerce has supplied a classification of the staff which it employed for the investigation of the financing of railroads (S. Res. 71, 74th Cong., 1st Sess.). The percentages were given for two stages in the inquiry:

	Dec. 1936	Dec. 1938
Attorneys	19%	21%
Research-Statistical	9%	4½%
Examiner-Accountant	30%	4½%
Clerical	42%	51%
Editorial	—	7%
Indexers	—	12%

Mr. Telford Taylor, a member of the staff, explained: " You will note that the principal change has been the pronounced reduction in the number of examiner-accountants on the staff. This is chiefly due to the fact that during 1938 the staff completed the bulk of the field work which it had undertaken, and the need for examiners was correspondingly lessened." (Letter to the writer, April 19, 1939).

[40] See *infra*, p. 108, footnote.

junction to restrain the committee, decided to appeal. The chairman thereupon introduced a joint resolution approving $10,000 for the hire of counsel to defend the committee's position; [41] but the House rejected it by a vote of 153 to 137. This slap supposedly was prompted, in part at least, by the previous activities of the investigators. The committee had, for instance, intimated that several members of the House received favors from lobbyists, and had conflicted with a committee of the House in obtaining the testimony of H. C. Hopson of the Associated Gas & Electric Co.[42] Several Democratic Representatives, moreover, resented the attempt to draw their party into the Senate committee's controversy. The Senate, however, by a new simple resolution,[43] approved the hire, exempt from the legal limitation, of Crampton Harris, the former legal partner of Chairman Black.

The $3,600 restriction, however, was discarded for all committees by the seventy-fifth Congress. A proviso was substituted which stipulated that " the rate of compensation for any position under the appropriations now available for, or herein or hereafter made for, expenses of inquiries and investigations of the Senate or expenses of special and select committees of the House of Representatives shall not exceed the rates fixed under the Classification Act of 1923, as amended, for positions

[41] S. J. Res. 234, 74th Cong., 2d Sess.

[42] See *supra*, p. 39, footnote.

[43] S. Res. 286, 74th Cong., 2d Sess., June 6, 1936, which provided: " Resolved, That the Senate ratifies and confirms the action of the special Senate committee in the employment of Crampton Harris as attorney to represent the Senate in the suit filed by William Randolph Hearst in the Supreme Court of the District of Columbia against the special Senate committee . . . Resolved, That the Senate Committee to Audit and Control the Contingent Expenses of the Senate is hereby authorized to fix the amount of the fee to be paid the said Crampton Harris for representing the Senate in the said Supreme Court of the District of Columbia and any other courts to which said case may be taken by appeal or otherwise . . . Resolved, That the said Committee to Audit and Control the Contingent Expenses of the Senate is authorized to provide for payment of the expenses necessarily incurred in connection with such litigation, . . . out of the appropriation for miscellaneous items of the contingent fund of the Senate."

with comparable duties; and the salary limitations of $3,600 attached to the appropriations heretofore made for expenses of inquiries and investigations of the Senate or for expenses of special and select committees of the House of Representatives are hereby repealed." [44] It is probably safe to say that a $3,600-a-year limit on salaries is bound to cripple some committees. Proceeding, as they frequently must, against groups who are represented by some of the most handsomely paid legal men in the country, it approaches the ridiculous to expect a committee to find competent help among the seventy-dollar-a-week class. Wisdom prescribes a limit at some point, however. The desirability of the new formula over the old seems to be unquestionable.

The almost universal practice is to ignore the requirements of the Civil Service in choosing personnel. The contention sometimes heard that " you can't examine a man to be a fact finder " carries the unconvincing ring of a convenient excuse; but the procedure probably is justified in the light of the temporary character of such positions.

In the past, established business agencies have sometimes been employed by committees. Senator Fletcher's group early made use of a firm of accountants for gathering statistics. But the practice is rare. The expense is a deterring influence as well as the possible anomaly of having business investigate business.

One of the principal reservoirs of staff material has been the administrative agencies. Partly to offset appropriations which committees consider too low, personnel is borrowed from the various executive bodies. A committee, of course, may obtain help without a complete transfer of personnel. The administrative agencies do, on occasion, gather facts for committees. Or the executive bodies may have on hand information of value. The LaFollette committee investigating violations of civil liberties was in touch with about thirty such

[44] 50 Stat. 9, February 9, 1937. The salary limitation is thus raised to $9,000. *Congressional Record*, 75th Cong., 1st Sess., p. 962, February 8, 1937.

agencies before it began its hearings. But beyond this, a committee may obtain the full-time services of permanent civil servants. Thus, the House committee studying the petroleum industry in 1934 [45] used twelve employees from the Bureau of Mines and other divisions of the Department of Interior. A report [46] of the committee probing real estate bondholders' reorganizations testified to the cooperation of the Securities and Exchange Commission which had lent a technical adviser; also assigned to the committee for a short period were thirty of the staff of the Bureau of Internal Revenue. And the subcommittee of the House Committee on Military Affairs which was inquiring into alleged irregularities in the War Department [47] expressed its appreciation of the aid given by employees of the Bureau of Internal Revenue, and by attorneys and accountants from the Comptroller General's office.[48] Not uncommonly the authorizing resolution may direct such assistance. The Department of Justice, for example, was requested to furnish to the Senate committee investigating the administration of justice in the courts " such investigators and legal assistants as the committee may require." [49] Although the resolution directing the 1937 inquiry into the problems of unemployment and relief contained no such stipulation, a second resolution which increased the committee's membership also granted it permission " to call upon the executive departments for clerical and other assistants." [50] And, to cite one more example, the resolution in 1938 which authorized the funds for the committee of the House investigating un-American activities provided that "the head of each executive department is hereby requested to detail to said special committee such number of legal and expert assistants and investigators as said committee may from time

[45] H. Res. 441, 73d Cong., 2d Sess., June 15, 1934.
[46] H. Rept. 35, 74th Cong., 1st Sess., January 29, 1935.
[47] H. Res. 275, 73d Cong., 2d Sess., March 2, 1934.
[48] H. Rept. 4, 74th Cong., 1st Sess., January 4, 1935.
[49] S. Res. 170, 74th Cong., 1st Sess., July 25, 1935.
[50] S. Res. 145, 75th Cong., 1st Sess., July 22, 1937.

to time deem necessary." [51] One house of Congress is without the power directly to enforce compliance with such orders. It may compel action, however, by means of the pressure which it is able to exert as a result of its control over appropriations. The committee on " un-Americanism ", complaining of a lack of cooperation by various agencies, pleaded, by means of a resolution of the committee and a letter to the President, for assistance.[52] But the House at that time showed little inclination to offer support to the committee's request, probably due, in part at least, to the apparent efforts of the committee to discredit the New Deal.

The lending of personnel, whether directed or voluntary, is not a new custom, but its extent since 1933 would seem indicative of a relatively close bond between the legislative and executive branches of the federal government. From an individual viewpoint the possible value to a civil servant of a " sabbatical spree " must be admitted. Employees can be materially benefitted by fresh outlooks from points outside their accustomed confines.[53] But the weakness of the borrowing procedure from a supervisory point of view led to a move for its curtailment in the seventy-fifth Congress. A number of the administrators

[51] H. Res. 510, 75th Cong., 3d Sess., June 9, 1938.

[52] *New York Times*, August 24, 1938.

[53] The following bit of Congressional debate by Representative Woodrum, however, illustrates why a straddling of duties may be inadvisable: " I want to say that all too frequently service on Capitol Hill almost disqualifies him for doing effective work down in the department again . . . I will tell why. In a specific instance an agent was detailed from one of the departments for six, seven, or eight months to aid an investigating committee. The committee to which he was detailed needed his services periodically. His bureau then could not keep him. He would report to Capitol Hill instead of to the bureau where he was employed. When asked by his superior in the department: 'How about doing a little job for us today?' he would reply ' Jim '—calling the distinguished Senator by his first name—' said for me to see him about a very important matter. I will see about that, and I will come down later. Tomorrow I have to have lunch with Tom and a crowd of the boys; we have got to consult about an important matter ', and so on, and so forth. In other words, if he does not watch out, he gets a little too Congressional for departmental work. It is not fair to the department." *Congressional Record*, 75th Cong., 1st Sess., p. 3395, April 12, 1937.

of relief had been lent to various Congressional investigating committees. A report for January 1937 alone placed the figure at twenty-six with annual salaries totaling $61,420.[54] The protests concerning the practice centered on two disadvantages: (1) Congress could have only a limited knowledge of, and control over, an investigating committee's total expenses; (2) the departments and agencies, to justify larger appropriations, were pointing to the expensive assistance given to committees. Under pressure from the House, therefore, the Senate was induced to accept a proviso in the first deficiency appropriation bill, which contained a large allotment for relief, that after thirty days no part of the funds should be used " to pay the compensation of any person, not taken from relief rolls, detailed or loaned for service in connection with any investigation or inquiry undertaken by any committee of either house of Congress under special resolution thereof." [55] As a result, the LaFollette committee lost a considerable block of its personnel. Senator Wheeler's committee investigating the financing of railroads also suffered withdrawals. The latter committee employed a rough total of one hundred and twenty-five persons, not more than half of whom were on the committee's payroll. Perhaps one-third were borrowed from the Interstate Commerce Commission. This committee was again seriously threatened, therefore, when the House included a stipulation in the independent offices appropriation bill of June 28, 1937 [56] that " None of the funds herein appropriated for any executive department or other executive agency shall be available to pay any compensation or other expense in connection with any investigation or inquiry under a resolution of either house of Congress." The Senate was successful in eliminating this proviso, however, in conference.[57]

[54] *Congressional Record*, 75th Cong., 1st Sess., p. 460, January 26, 1937.

[55] 50 Stat. 10, February 9, 1937.

[56] 50 Stat. 329, June 28, 1937.

[57] Sec. 3678 of the Revised Statutes also has been cited in Congressional debate, although without much effect, as a possible deterrent to such borrow-

CHARTING THE COMMITTEE'S PROCEDURE. With the staff assembled, the task remains of determining how best to collect the needed information. Contrary to the general impression, the public hearings bring forth little new material; they are a means, rather, of floodlighting the facts already gathered. The greater part of the information is often obtained by long and wearying hours of poring over files. A trained personnel is needed for this step. Corporations, frequent objects of inquiry, yield baffling financial records which only accountants can fathom. Legal problems are presented which only lawyers can solve. Even the perusal of bulky files of day-to-day correspondence can become an art; an investigator grows expert at quickly noting the pertinent paragraphs. A realization by Senator Nye that probing can be developed into a skill was indicated by his request for the use in his munitions inquiry of employees of the Interstate Commerce Commission who were just finishing work for the Senate committee investigating the air mail contracts.[58]

Speaking generally, this first line of offense of an investigating committee meets inconsequential opposition. On isolated occasions a wholesale destruction of records before a committee has begun its activities has frustrated the acquisition of pertinent evidence. The recoil of suspicions thus engendered can be so damaging, however, that cooperation rather than recusancy by persons being investigated has been the rule.[59]

Currently, one of the chief legal obstacles encountered by committees results from a provision in the law covering the contumacy of witnesses. Section 102 of the Revised Statutes[60]

ing: "All sums appropriated for various branches of expenditure in public service shall be applied solely to the object for which they are respectively made, and for no other." See the remarks of Representative Woodrum, *Congressional Record*, 75th Cong., 1st Sess., p. 3395, April 12, 1937.

[58] S. Res. 349, 72d Cong., 2d Sess., February 25, 1933.

[59] The coöperation is frequently genuine, but it is sometimes fostered by the reluctance of the courts to restrain Congressional committees. See Chapter V.

[60] Sections 101, 102, 103, 104 and 859 of the Revised Statutes, all relating

provides, in part, that " Every person who having been summoned as a witness by the authority of either House of Congress to give testimony or to produce papers upon any matter under inquiry before either House, or any joint committee established by a joint or concurrent resolution of the two Houses of Congress, or any committee of either House of Congress, wilfully makes default, or who, having appeared, refuses to answer any question pertinent to the question under inquiry, shall be deemed guilty of a misdemeanor." Because this applies to contumacy before only a house of Congress or the members of one of its committees and not before the members of a committee's staff making inspections in the field, Senator Fletcher sponsored an amendment in the seventy-fourth Congress which would have tightened the statute.[61] But only eleven days after his explanation of the proviso on the floor of the Senate, the Senator was dead, and no member

to the power of Congressional committees to examine witnesses, were amended by 52 Stat. 942, June 13, 1938, in order to give joint committees the same powers as committees of either the House or Senate. U. S. Code, Title 2, sections 191, 192, 193, 194; and Title 28, sec. 634.

61 Senator Fletcher's proposal, offered in the form of an amendment to H. R. 8875, provided that " Every person who (a) having been summoned as a witness by the authority of either House of Congress to give testimony upon any matter which is under inquiry by either House or by any committee or subcommittee of either House of Congress wilfully makes default or (b) having appeared refuses to answer any question pertinent to the matter under inquiry or (c) after service upon him of a subpoena issued by authority of either House in connection with such inquiry (1) fails to permit examination as requested by such subpoena by either House or by any committee or subcommittee of either House, *or by a duly authorized agent of such House, committee, or subcommittee* (italics not in the original), of such books, records, papers, documents, or correspondence in his possession, custody or control as such House, committee or subcommittee has reason to believe may be pertinent to the inquiry, or (2) fails to produce and deliver to, or fails to permit to be copied by such House, committee, subcommittee, or agent any books, records, papers, documents, or correspondence in his possession, custody, or control which are pertinent to such inquiry, as required by such subpoena, shall be deemed guilty of a misdemeanor punishable by a fine of not more than $1,000 nor less than $100 and imprisonment in a common jail for not less than 1 month nor more than 12 months." *Congressional Record*, 74th Cong., 2d Sess., p. 9147, June 6, 1936.

deigned to wage battle for his amendment. A bill pertaining to investigations was enacted,[62] but minus the Fletcher provision, and no concerted drive has been made since to effect the change. Meanwhile, in practice, committees have sometimes sidestepped the obstacle by threatening burdensome subpoenas. Corporations, reluctant to permit as free access to their files as a committee's investigators may request, may grow more amenable when faced with the expense and trouble of transporting to Washington " a whole trainload of papers." [63]

One possible aid to all investigators is the questionnaire. Such groups as the Senate lobbying committee of 1935 and the House committee studying real estate bondholders' protective committees were successful in gathering worthwhile information by means of a series of questions sent to rather large mailing lists. The value of this device, however, can be easily overrated. It is not practicable for delving into deeply hidden facts which those who are being investigated may wish to suppress. Carefully considered replies may simulate complete answers, but may be only evasions or half truths. The use of questionnaires, moreover, is hardly suitable for throwing much light on particularly intricate problems. The Federal Trade Commission, for instance, after its efforts to obtain data by this means on the financial development and management of the electric utilities, came to the conclusion that " it was

[62] 49 Stat. 2041, July 13, 1936 (H. R. 8875, 74th Cong.), which removed one impediment to the committees investigating between Congressional sessions. Previously it had been necessary for the Senate or the House to be in session before a committee could start criminal proceedings against a recalcitrant witness. The new provision permits the Vice-President or the Speaker of the House, as the case may be, to certify charges of contumacy to the appropriate federal attorney when Congress is not in session. The law was used for the first time by the subcommittee of the Senate Committee on Education and Labor investigating violations of civil liberties, when, two months after the adjournment of Congress, it asked for the indictment of witnesses who failed to appear in response to subpoenas. L. Douglas Rice and W. Boone Groves were tried by a jury in the District Court of the District of Columbia on May 18 and 19, 1937 and were acquitted.

[63] Black, op. cit.

impracticable to get a reasonably informative report by questionnaire on such varied and complicated transactions." [64]

In investigations of a more educational rather than an in-
quisitorial nature, wide use may be made of general research.
Experts in specific fields are called on for treatises. Senator
Aldrich's Monetary Commission of 1908 [65] immersed itself in
a galaxy of studies specially prepared by economists and finan-
ciers. Professor O. M. W. Sprague, for example, wrote on the
" History of Crises under the National Banking System ";
Paul M. Warburg on " The Discount System in Europe ";
Francis W. Hirst, editor of " The Economist ", on " The
Credit of Nations "; and other foreign experts contributed
studies of the banks of their respective nations. The House
Interstate and Foreign Commerce committee also made use of a
specialist when, having been ordered to analyze the ownership
and control of the railroads,[66] it issued a three-volume study,
" Regulation of Stock Ownership in Railroads ", prepared
under the direction of its counsel, Walter M. W. Splawn.[67]
The same Mr. Splawn, incidentally, was responsible for a comprehensive report on pipe lines issued under the auspices of a
committee investigating the ownership by holding companies
of public utility corporations.[68] A few months later the House
committee on the Post Office and Post Roads which was probing
the expenditures of the Post Office Department,[69] commissioned Dr. J. B. Crane of Harvard to study the airmail service.
And the Senate and House committees which were considering
the reorganization of the administration of the federal gov-

[64] S. Doc. 92, 70th Cong., 1st Sess., part 72A, p. 20.

[65] 35 Stat. 552.

[66] H. Res. 114, 71st Cong., 2d Sess., January 24, 1930; H. Rept. 2789,
71st Cong., 3d Sess.

[67] He was appointed to the Interstate Commerce Commission in 1934.

[68] H. Res. 59, 72d Cong., 1st Sess., January 19, 1932; H. Rept. 2192,
72d Cong., 2d Sess.

[69] H. Res. 226, 72d Cong., 1st Sess., June 21, 1932; H. Rept. 2087,
72d Cong., 2d Sess.

ernment [70] relied in large part on studies by the Brookings Institution. Other examples of the use of specialists by committees can be cited, but the broad assertion may nevertheless be made that detached experts are not employed by Congressional investigating committees to the extent which their value seems to justify.

Some investigating bodies have used income tax returns. On occasion, commissions, as well as Congressional committees, have been granted the privilege of access to the figures. For its inquiry into the agricultural income, the Federal Trade Commission was given " the same right to obtain data and to inspect income tax returns as the Committee on Ways and Means of the House of Representatives or the Committee on Finance of the Senate." [71] And in its investigation of the utilities, the Federal Trade Commission verified some of its evidence by comparing it with information gleaned from income tax returns. But no authority for an access to the returns can be given at the time of the creation of most committees, since they are established by a resolution of only one house of Congress. Although a joint resolution [72] was passed directing the Treasury Department to make available, to the Senate committee investigating the stock exchanges, all income tax returns which the committee might request, such a privilege, if considered advisable, is customarily conferred by an executive order. Thus the President retains the power to add sharp teeth to an investigation. The grant is infrequently made. The Dies committee studying " un-American " propaganda was one recipient of the power.[73] An executive order [74] also conferred on

[70] S. Res. 217, 74th Cong., 2d Sess., February 24, 1936; H. Res. 460, 74th Cong., 2d Sess., April 29, 1936. •

[71] 49 Stat. 931, August 27, 1935.

[72] 47 Stat. 708, July 19, 1932.

[73] Executive Order No. 7933A, July 14, 1938; *Federal Register* of August 9, 1938.

[74] Executive Order No. 7869, April 18, 1938; *Federal Register* of April 20, 1938.

the Senate committee investigating lobbying the authority to inspect any income tax returns; this action hinted more at politics, however, since the order was issued in 1938, in the heat of the battle over administrative reorganization in the federal government, when the committee was investigating the organized efforts to defeat the President's plan. It would seem to be in accordance with sound judgment that this power to inspect returns is infrequently given, since it is easily susceptible to abuse by committees. The American Civil Liberties Union showed concern over the possibilities of its misuse, by issuing a statement after the Presidential grant to the committee on lobbying: "When subpoenas are served on individuals for income tax returns or any financial records they may be resisted by appeal to the courts, . . . But when income tax returns are made available by the Treasury Department no protection by resort to the courts is afforded to citizens. The procedure cannot be challenged except by public protest. We desire to enter our protest with you against your use of information obtained other than by subpoenas. It is a procedure out of line with the spirit, if not the letter, of our constitutional guarantees." [75] It should be borne in mind, however, that the grant of the power is, in some cases, probably essential to the conduct of a thorough investigation.

HEARINGS: PURPOSE.   Because most inquiries may thrive or decay on the basis of the care taken with the vital preparation prior to the hearings, well-managed investigations generally reach the public hearings stage only after extensive preliminaries. The interval between the adoption of the resolution and the hearings varies widely. The thoroughness of the preparation cannot be judged alone, however, by the elapsed time. The committees do not always swing into action immediately upon the passage of a resolution. Moreover, some committees may have material already gathered before an investigation is authorized. The possible wide variations are

[75] Letter of May 27, 1938 to Chairman Minton.

suggested by the Senate committee investigating railroad financing [76] which did not begin its hearings for a year and a half; and the Senate committee of 1935 inquiring into lobbying [77] which listened to testimony one day after its authorization.

The public hearings of the Congressional investigations, in general, serve two principal purposes. They may, on the one hand, act as a check on the investigators. If no hearings are conducted, or if they are of a private nature, the persons who are under investigation may have little opportunity to present their case; the public hearings are sometimes desirable, therefore, because, since they permit an airing of conflicting views,[78] they may be one means of bringing about an equitable inquiry. The hearings are, in the second place, utilized by the committees to throw the light of publicity on the findings and to mould public opinion.[79] Not infrequently the quantity of new material unearthed in the hearings is insignificant. Indeed, a few committees have adopted the method of holding preliminary private hearings to determine the relevancy of the proposed testimony. In the commission field, the Securities and Exchange Commission has gone so far as to conduct prior hearings in executive session in order to avoid the pitfalls of impromptu public questionings.

If the usual procedure is followed, field men or questionnaires or other research activities first provide the committees with facts. But the chairmen think that the facts must be presented dramatically to the public. The hearings provide the means. The witnesses are interrogated on the contents of correspondence already collected by the committee, and are asked

[76] S. Res. 71, 74th Cong., 1st Sess., May 20, 1935.

[77] S. Res. 165, 74th Cong., 1st Sess., July 11, 1935.

[78] Although the witnesses before the Congressional investigating committees not uncommonly complain that they have an insufficient chance to present their viewpoints, it is probably safe to say that only in rare instances is a witness deprived of the opportunity at least to voice a grievance.

[79] See *supra*, p. 30.

to read aloud their own telegrams handed to them by inquiring
Congressmen. On occasion, such correspondence may not por-
tray a complete picture. Then may the examination of witnesses
elicit connecting bits of information. But the value of these
extractions alone would not warrant most hearings.

PROCEDURE IN HEARINGS.   The procedure employed in the
hearings, perhaps more than any other aspect of investigations,
has been the object of criticism both by witnesses and by outside observers. It must be admitted that, in many instances,
the hearings can by no means be considered as models of an
effective examination of witnesses, and that the tone of the
proceedings often leaves much to be desired. Too frequently
the investigators have ignored the need for a careful preparation. The hearings are impromptu. The questioners are ill-
informed. The witnesses, because the examination is fumbling,
are the more willing to risk being held in contempt of the
committee. They resort, therefore, to persiflage, and they
parry the questions. Indeed, some of the inanities in the records
of the hearings are incredible. They have to be seen to be believed. The hearings conducted by the Senate committee investigating lobbying in 1935, for example, contribute a number
of illustrations of the imperfections which are found all too
frequently in Congressional inquiries. Thus, Chairman Black
was quizzing Vance Muse, the state director of the Texas Tax
Relief Committee and also " connected with " the Southern
Committee to Uphold the Constitution:

> The Chairman.   You may be seated, Mr. Muse.
> Mr. Muse.   Senator, may I stand?
> The Chairman.   Certainly, if you prefer.
> Mr. Muse.   I think I should stand in the presence of the Senate
> of the United States, in which I have implicit faith.
>
> .   .   .   .
>
> The Chairman (referring to the Texas committee).   Your as-
> sociation has been running for four and a half years?
> Mr. Muse.   Yes.
> The Chairman.   When did it start?

Mr. Muse. Don't get me mixed up on dates; four and a half years; if I miss it fifteen days is it going to hurt me?

The Chairman. Maybe not, not if you do it honestly.

Mr. Muse. I will tell you what we did—

The Chairman (interposing). All we want, Mr. Muse, in order to make it clear so that there will be no misunderstanding, we want the truth, and there is not any need for quips, or anything of that kind.

Mr. Muse. I never lied in my life, even to my wife.

The Chairman. All right. When was the organization started?

Mr. Muse. It is a funny arrangement there—

The Chairman (interposing). When did it start?

Mr. Muse. About four and a half years ago. When did we get this fool amendment out of the Federal Constitution (addressing Mr. Kirby)?

The Chairman. When did it start is the question I asked. I didn't ask for the other.

Mr. Muse. Well—

The Chairman (interposing). That is the question I asked, a very simple question.

Mr. Muse. What organization are you talking about?

The Chairman. The tax league which you mentioned.

Mr. Muse. That was four years and a half ago. You ought to know from a calendar when it is.

The Chairman. Well, about what date?

Mr. Muse. Have we got one of those Senate calendars around here?

The Chairman. Do you know about what date, or do you not know? If you do not know, then say so.

Mr. Muse. If you will give me the privilege of looking at a calendar I will tell you exactly when the organization was formed.

The Chairman. We will pass on from that, and you will have an opportunity to look at a calendar. When did you go with the other organization, the Southern—

Mr. Muse (interposing). Now I want to say this—

The Chairman (interposing). You stop that.

Mr. Muse. Why should I stop?

The Chairman. You stop until we ask you a question. If you have come here with the idea you are going to make statements about anything in the world you please, or about everything in the world you think about, which is wholly immaterial and irrelevant to the question asked and to the resolution—

Mr. Muse (interposing). But you are putting a strain on my feeble mind, and I can't answer.

The Chairman (continuing). Then we want to disabuse your mind.

Mr. Muse. What do you want me to answer?

The Chairman. We want you to answer the questions. We are going to treat you with courtesy, and we expect you to follow the same course.

Mr. Muse. That will be an innovation here, but we will try it.

The Chairman. Mr. Muse, if you make any more statements of that type, which are wholly uncalled for—you have been treated with the utmost courtesy—it may be you want to go before a Senate committee,[80] I do not know; it may be that would be a wise plan.

Mr. Muse. That would be an honor anyway.

The Chairman. If it is, your wishes will be granted if you do not answer the questions properly.

Mr. Muse. Do you mean to go before the bar of the Senate? I am in a daze here; I am excited.

The Chairman. I mean we are going to ask you questions, Mr. Muse, and we are going to ask them courteously, with reference to the matters which the committee is investigating. And we expect answers. And if you do not know you can so state. And if you do know you can state so. The question asked you was when did you go with the Southern Committee to Uphold the Constitution? It is a very simple question.

Mr. Muse. Well I didn't know—

The Chairman (interposing). Do you know?

---

[80] The Senator may have meant to say "before the bar of the Senate." Although the stenographic record of a committee's hearings usually could be improved tremendously by extensive corrections and reductions, few committees have adopted this practice. The Royal Commissions of inquiry in England, on the other hand, not infrequently submit proofs of the stenographers' notes to both the questioners and the witnesses who can and do make alterations; the possible abuses of this procedure are obvious, however.

Mr. Muse.   There has been a misunderstanding.   I didn't know what organization you were talking about.

The Chairman.   Do you know when you went with them or not?

Mr. Muse.   I do know.

The Chairman.   When was that?

Mr. Muse.   You didn't ask the question plainly.

The Chairman.   Do you know or do you not?

Mr. Muse.   I do.

The Chairman.   All right, when was it?

Mr. Muse.   It was when it was formulated.   When was it, Governor, we formulated that thing?

Mr. Kirby.   July 1935.[81]

One of the instances of the evasiveness of Howard Hopson, of the Associated Gas and Electric system, also may be cited from the same heairngs:

The Chairman.   Mr. Hopson, do you know whether or not Mr. Robinson, during the time he was here, was dealing in buying and selling stocks or bonds or debentures of the Associated Gas & Electric or its associates?

Mr. Hopson.   He is in the securities business, and I assume that his firm carried on their business the same as they would under any other conditions.

The Chairman.   Do I understand that you do not know whether he was dealing in buying and selling, on the market, debentures and bonds and stocks of the Associated Gas?

Mr. Hopson.   I think he very likely did.

The Chairman.   You know he was, don't you Mr. Hopson?

Mr. Hopson.   No; I do not have any personal knowledge of it whatsoever. How could I know, Senator?

---

[81] *Investigation of Lobbying Activities.* Hearings Before a Special Committee to Investigate Lobbying Activities, United States Senate, 74th and 75th Congresses, Pursuant to S. Res. 165 and S. Res. 184 (74th Congress), 8 parts, p. 1963. A striking contrast to the general tone of these hearings is afforded, for example, by the orderly examination of a contumacious witness by the select committee which investigated the Marconi scandal in England in 1912-13. See the " Special Report (no. 515) from the Select Committee on Marconi's Wireless Telegraph Company, Limited, Agreement," February 12, 1913, *Parliamentary Papers*, 1912-13, vol. viii.

The Chairman. You are sure, absolutely sure now, as I understand it, that you did not know it?

Mr. Hopson. Even if he told me so, I would not know of it of my own knowledge. You are asking me—

The Chairman (interposing). Did he tell you so?

Mr. Hopson. He may have.

Senator Schwellenbach. Mr. Chairman, I call your attention to that answer, that even if this man told him what the matter was himself that he would not know of his own knowledge. The time has come that this witness has to answer the questions and not argue.

The Chairman. Mr. Hopson, when I ask a question, of course, we do not assume that you will be so technical in the construction of what I am asking you; and what I was asking you was whether or not—I will change that question so as to meet it. Have you or not been informed that during the time Mr. Robinson was here he was dealing in stocks of the Associated Gas . . . or any of its associates or affiliates or subsidiaries or holding companies or relatives?

Mr. Hopson. My opinion is, and I think I have been informed, that he carried on a very active business in buying and selling securities of the Associated Gas & Electric System.[82]

Both the investigator and the investigated too frequently fail to remember that the hearings should not be used as platforms for political speeches. Patrick J. Hurley, a former Republican Secretary of War, for instance, requested and was granted the permission to testify in the same inquiry. The members of the committee and the witness approached the session fully prepared for warfare. The parting shots of a fatuous exchange ran as follows:

Mr. Hurley. Senator then may I close—would you be offended if I would close with this suggestion?

The Chairman. This is not a quotation from any poet? You can sit down and do it.

Mr. Hurley. I suggest to this committee and to all of—

82 Hearings, p. 1199.

The Chairman. Wave the other hand, too.

Mr. Hurley (continuing)—and to all my friends of the opposition that they read Dean Swift's Gulliver's Travels and the Man Who Corrupted Hadleyburg, by Mark Twain, and when they have read that, if they have done that, let them read the Golden Rule according to St. Matthew. I thank you.

The Chairman. Can you not quote a little poetry at the end? [83]

The members of the committees at times engage in ill-advised political wranglings among themselves. In the same inquiry into lobbying, Senator Gibson, a Republican, habitually found himself unable to suppress side remarks. For example, while a witness explained why he had paid an agent a weekly retaining fee of one hundred dollars for practically no duties, the Senator intervened: " You must be a New Dealer; paying out money for doing nothing." [84] Partisan thrusts may find a justification on the floor of Congress, but nothing is gained by their inclusion in an investigation's hearings. The inquiry into the Tennessee Valley Authority suffered from intra-committee skirmishes, mostly between Republicans and Democrats, which became a part of the record and were featured in the newspaper reports of the hearings. Proceedings marked by a committee clearly divided into critics and defenders of those on the witness stand are not conducive to an effective investigation. [85]

It should be added to any discussion of the procedure employed in the hearings that an investigating committee may, to some extent, determine the privileges to be accorded to the witneses appearing before it. Thus, the customary practice of most Congressional investigators is to allow the witnesses the privilege of presenting prepared statements preparatory to the

[83] Hearings, p. 857.

[84] Hearings, p. 1539.

[85] It should be mentioned, in passing, that the physical surroundings of some hearings are a handicap to the committees. A general bustle, coupled, perhaps, with the poor acoustics of the hearing room, does not promote orderliness.

general questioning.[86] Some of these manuscripts, however, have needlessly consumed valuable time in the hearings. The statements, prepared with the help of lawyers and publicity agents, have often been designed to sway public opinion by declarations and statistics having little relevance to the issue at hand. Moreover, sugar-coated platitudes have tended to detract from the effectiveness of the later revelations. One commentator has issued a warning that "The investigator who lets an investigated magnate read an opening statement is falling easy prey to what is now a very obvious stratagem." [87] Some committees have, therefore, "in order to expedite matters," refused to witnesses the privilege of presenting prepared statements. Nevertheless, despite the drawbacks, the granting of the privilege in most instances seems to be essential to equitableness. If the witnesses are allowed to make only direct answers to specific questions, important gaps in the testimony may result.

In courtroom procedure, cross-examination affords an opportunity for the presentation of all the pertinent facts. The current custom in the majority of investigations is, however, to permit little or no cross-examination.[88] This practice is supported by the reasoning that investigations are not trials, that courtroom procedure, if applied to Congressional inquiries, might well hamper them so seriously as to defeat their purpose. It would seem, however, that a committee should proceed with caution in deciding that it will not allow cross-examination. Felix Frankfurter, although urging "hands off the investigations" and declaring himself to be generally opposed to a revision of the procedure employed in the inquiries, nevertheless maintains that "Of course, the essential decencies must be observed, namely opportunity for cross-examination must be afforded to those who are investigated or to those representing

[86] The reading of these prepared statements may or may not be interrupted by interrogations which are aimed at clarification.

[87] John T. Flynn, 89 *New Republic* 74 (1936).

[88] Most committees recognize that witnesses are entitled to consult counsel.

issues under investigation." [89] The discussion of the problem of cross-examination is linked to some extent with that of prepared statements. A witness, both by cross-examination and by inserting a prepared statement in the record, may counteract baseless innuendoes. On occasion, a committee's prohibition of one of these privileges may be warranted in the interests of the inquiry's efficiency. An undue effort to " expedite matters," however, would seem to be chargeable to a committee, such as the one investigating lobbying in 1935, which banned prepared statements [90] and at the same time gave to witnesses little or no opportunity for cross-examination.[91] Moreover, a committee's refusal, whether apparent or real, to hear all the aspects of a subject under inquiry helps to lessen the public's confidence in the investigators' conclusions.

It should be stressed, in conclusion, that although a wide variety of examples can be cited of imperfections in the hearings, and of downright abuses by both the investigator and the investigated, they must not be understood as habitual. The excerpts offered from the hearings of the committee investigating lobbying are chosen as typical of one aspect of the investigatory process, but not of Congressional inquiry as a whole. Pages upon pages of solid testimony, pertinent but not startling, pass unnoticed by casual observers and unrecorded by news correspondents. It seems fair to say that on a consolidated balance sheet for all Congressional investigations, the asset of orderliness outweighs the liability of abuse.

AN INVESTIGATION MAY PROVIDE AN ANTI-CLIMAX. One further aspect of procedure deserves special mention. Both before and during the hearings, it behooves Congressional committees, in the interests of an effective inquiry, to guard carefully against an anti-climax. Because the moulding of general opinion is so important a purpose of many investigations, all the available tools are utilized for arousing the public. The

[89] " Hands Off the Investigations," 38 New Republic 329 (1924).
[90] Hearings, p. 835.
[91] See, for example, the Hearings, p. 1469.

scheme of some committees to plan at least one news-worthy disclosure each day during the hearings has frequently received comment from critics who are convinced that the members predominantly seek personal publicity. Moreover, even before an inquiry is authorized charges are sometimes made by the sponsors of the resolution in order to insure its approval, and statements are issued to sharpen the public's appetite for the revelation of information. But the technique may be overdone. Thus, Representative Cochran, seeking additional funds for the Committee on Military Affairs to investigate the alleged profiteering and other irregularities in the War Department,[92] predicted: " a scandal that will arouse the people of the country and in all probability open the doors of penitentiaries to government officials will undoubtedly be the result of this investigation." [93] Although some irregularities were disclosed, their magnitude was dwarfed by the anticipation.[94]

A less conscious contribution to anti-climactic impressions may come from the seeming propensity of Senators and Representatives to employ a prosecuting attorney's technique of inquisition. That Congress is heavily weighted by lawyers is well known. That many politicians have begun their careers in the county prosecutor's office also has been established.[95] A respectable portion of the members of Congress therefore find themselves on familiar ground when pointing accusing fingers. A comment concerning Senator Thomas J. Walsh, unjustifiably disparaging in view of the benefits resulting from his investigating, serves nevertheless to make the point: " (he) seems to find the same degree of pleasure in investigation that some men find in intoxication." [96]

---

[92] H. Res. 275, 73d Cong., 2d Sess., March 2, 1934.

[93] *Congressional Record*, 73d Cong., 2d Sess., p. 12118, June 16, 1934.

[94] See *supra*, p. 36.

[95] Raymond Moley, *Politics and Criminal Prosecution* (New York, Minton, Balch & Co., 1929).

[96] Senator William C. Bruce, *Congressional Record*, 70th Cong., 1st Sess., p. 3006, February 15, 1928.

The tendency of some inquiries to lose effectiveness through an excess of promotion may at times be the result of " devil hunting." Accusations of " devil " or " witch " hunting are hurled at one time or another against most muckraking investigations. Congressmen are accused of magnifying their personal antipathies in order to force an investigation, and of fashioning straw devils as a justification for elaborate probing. Evidence, if needed, of a wide distrust of the intentions of investigators was afforded by the frequency of Chairman O'Mahoney's statements in defense of the " monopoly " investigation; weeks before the hearings had begun, he was assuring the public that the inquiry was " not a witch hunt," and " not a punitive inquiry," and had " no intention to pillory industry." The critics of investigations, prone to follow their general sympathies, too frequently fail, when drawing conclusions, to distinguish between the genuine satans and those preconceived in the minds of Congressmen. The latter, by no means in the majority during the last decade, unfortunately tend to be emphasized by the critics to the benefit of the former. Sometimes, however, the devils are created as a result of the failure of the investigators to perceive that the social or economic systems, rather than one or a specific group of individuals, are responsible for the particular ills. An inquiry, therefore, may aim to expose a personal devil when, in reality, the causes lie deeper. Thus, the repeated probings of the declines in the prices of cotton,[97] insofar as they tended to lay the blame on single individuals, appear to be rather futile. The inquiry into the munitions industry [98] was another example of an investigation which probably suffered from an anti-climax following a search for specific causes of war. Senator Nye and other supporters of the probe fully realized the desirability of shaping public opinion along lines sympathetic to the committee's work. The revelations were significant; a valuable store of historical documents was gathered for the enlightenment of coming generations;

[97] See *supra*, p. 47.
[98] S. Res. 206, 73d Cong., 2d Sess., April 12, 1934.

some of the activities behind the scenes during the World War were revealed to the nation. But the fanfare apparently had been too potent. The general public, keyed for more startling disclosures, scarcely could escape the disappointing conclusion that the country's general economic system had inevitably drawn the United States into the flames of war.[99] The dampened expectations led to a rather general attitude of ridicule. Thus, an experienced commentator like Paul Mallon was led to observe that "if all the data developed in the munitions investigation had been offered in a Senate speech by Chairman Nye, it would have received comparatively little attention." [100]

[99] See Charles A. Beard, *The Devil Theory of War* (New York, The Vanguard Press, 1936).

[100] *New York Times*, December 9, 1934.

CHAPTER IV
RESULTS

THE results of Congressional investigations are not always perceptible to the casual observer. A committee's accomplishments, it is true, may be easily traced when, after its study, it recommends measures which quickly become law. Likewise, the effects of a supervisory inquiry will be obvious if they lead to resignations or to disciplinary action in the executive branch of the government.

Many of the results, however, are not immediate, and many others are so indirect or abstract that their measurement is by no means easy. An inquiry may, for example, gather information which, although it is not used at once, may serve as a partial basis for legislation in later years. In any study of recent inquiries, of course, little evaluation can be made of the long time effects of investigations. An estimate of investigatory results is still more difficult because an important purpose of many inquiries is to mould public opinion. Thus, the investigators may aim to propel the public and the Congress into the support of a specific bill or of general legislation on a particular subject. Yet the actual effect of an investigation in shaping opinion can only be surmised. It is unquestionable, furthermore, that one fruit of investigations is that they help to restrain wrongdoing, both public and private; Representative McSwain, for example, voiced the obvious when he insisted: " It is not merely what Congress discovers that is the measure of the good done. It is the fact that Congress may investigate that restrains the ordinary impulse and tendency to corruption." [1] The threat of a possible Congressional inquiry undoubtedly serves, on occasion, as a check on individuals outside the government; and just as surely it is one of the safeguards against corruption in the administration. But any attempts to demonstrate that this threat prevents wrongdoing

[1] *Congressional Record*, 74th Cong., 1st Sess., p. 5508, April 12, 1935.

is doomed to at least partial failure. Moreover, the results of Congressional investigations also include action which other agencies of the government may take following the inquiries. Thus, the Department of Justice may initiate prosecutions on the basis of the facts which have been revealed by the committees. Likewise, the Treasury Department may take steps to recover taxes which the committees have shown were evaded.

Although an enumeration of the results of the investigations of the past decade can be only fragmentary, and although the accomplishments of a number of the individual investigations already have been treated, a panoramic view of some of the measurable results seems to be desirable.

From what has been said it should be clear that a mere compilation of the statutes which are enacted following the inquiries, although forming in many instances the only tangible yardstick of the results, is no fair criterion of the total effectiveness of investigations. Legislation, in fact, is not always intended. Nevertheless, it should be noted that several important laws of recent years can, in whole or in part, be traced directly to Congressional inquiries. The investigation by the Senate Banking and Currency Committee of stock exchanges and banking practices [2] may be singled out as the principal procreator of statutes. The committee's final report modestly observes that " during the progress of this investigation " there were enacted the banking act of 1933, the securities act of 1933, the securities exchange act of 1934, and " several amendments to the revenue act calculated to eliminate methods of tax avoidance described before the subcommittee." [3] While other circumstances and other investigations shared in bringing about the banking and the two securities bills, the Senate's inquiry played a predominant part. Moreover, further reforms were embodied in the banking act of 1935 which was approved after the submission of the committee's report. The personal effacements which befell leading bankers such as Messrs. Mitchell, Harri-

[2] S. Res. 84, 72d Cong., 1st Sess., March 4, 1932.
[3] S. Rept. 1455, 73d Cong., 2d Sess., June 16, 1934.

man, and Wiggin following the committee's disclosures [4] served to demonstrate that the results of an investigation may extend beyond the enactment of legislation.

Although most of the legislation suggested by the Senate munitions committee failed to be enacted, the inquiry was directly responsible for the neutrality act [5] which was forced through the Senate in the closing hours of the first session of the seventy-fourth Congress following the threat of a filibuster by the committee's chairman, Senator Nye.

The important indirect bearing on the public utility act of the Senate lobby committee's investigation has been cited in another connection.[6] The same success did not attend the committee's sponsorship of a bill requiring the registration of, and the filing of expense reports by, lobbyists. Both the Senate and the House passed bills along somewhat similar lines;[7] but the conference report was rejected by the House on June 17, 1936, only three days before the final adjournment of Congress, too late to permit further efforts at compromise.

Other examples of the more important statutes springing, at least in part, from recent investigations were: the air mail act of 1934, from the Senate committee investigating the air mail contracts;[8] the anti-price discrimination bill, from the House committee inquiring into the American Retail Federation;[9] an act regulating the payment of the " prevailing " rate of wages to the laborers on government construction work, from the Senate committee probing the " kick-back racket ";[10] eleven bills in the seventy-third Congress relating to crime, from a Senate committee investigating criminal practices;[11]

[4] See *supra*, p. 41.

[5] 49 Stat. 1081, August 31, 1935.

[6] See *supra*, p. 39.

[7] S. 2512 and H. R. 11663, 74th Cong.

[8] 48 Stat. 933; S. Res. 349, 72d Cong., 2d Sess., February 25, 1933.

[9] 49 Stat. 1526; H. Res. 203, 74th Cong., 1st Sess., April 24, 1935.

[10] 49 Stat. 1011; S. Res. 228, 73d Cong., 2d Sess., May 30, 1934.

[11] The bills are listed in S. Rept. 1440, 73d Cong., 2d Sess.; S. Res. 74, 73d Cong., 1st Sess., June 12, 1933.

four statutes concerning wild-life, from the Senate and House committees studying that subject; [12] an act to provide for the preservation of tin, from a House committee studying the supply of tin; [13] and the Johnson bill prohibiting loans to the countries which had defaulted on their debts, from the Senate committee investigating the sales of foreign securities in the United States. [14]

Beyond the immediate statutory results, however, an investigation may lay the groundwork for future legislative activities. Information may be accumulated to lie in storage until more opportune times. Reforms are not effected overnight. Piecemeal contributions to the general knowledge of unsatisfactory situations may eventually bear fruit. Thus, the hearings on crop insurance by a select committee of the Senate in 1923 [15] undoubtedly bore some relation to the creation of the Federal Crop Insurance Corporation in 1938. [16] And the Senate committee's study of unemployment insurance systems in the United States and foreign countries [17] in 1931 was one step toward the social security act of 1935. [18] Again, the suggestion by the 1934 House committee investigating foreign propaganda that all foreign political agents be required to register, [19] was adopted in 1938 [20] when the need seemed more acute. The possibility always remains, however, that the storehouses will be overlooked. In 1930, for instance, the Senate granted a select committee the authority to " investigate all matters pertaining to the replacement and conservation of wild animal life (includ-

[12] 48 Stat. 400, 401, 451, and 49 Stat. 378; S. Res. 246, 71st Cong., 2d Sess., April 17, 1930, and H. Res. 237, 73d Cong., 2d Sess., January 29, 1934.

[13] 49 Stat. 1140; H. Res. 404, 73d Cong., 2d Sess., June 15, 1934.

[14] 48 Stat. 574; S. Res. 19, 72d Cong., 1st Sess., December 10, 1931.

[15] S. Res. 341, 67th Cong., 2d Sess., September 9, 1922.

[16] 52 Stat. 31, February 16, 1938.

[17] S. Res. 483, 71st Cong., 3d Sess., February 28, 1931.

[18] 49 Stat. 620.

[19] H. Res. 198, 73d Cong., 2d Sess., March 20, 1934; see H. Rept. 153, 74th Cong., 1st Sess., February 15, 1935.

[20] 52 Stat. 631, June 8, 1938.

ing aquatic and bird life) with a view to determining the appropriate methods for carrying out such purposes." [21] Four years later, while the committee was still conducting hearings, a House group was chosen to " investigate all matters pertaining to the replacement and conservation of wild animal life (including aquatic and bird life) with a view to determining the most appropriate method of carrying out such purposes." [22] Although the second inquiry was justified, according to the sponsors, by its broader scope, the record reveals tendencies to an unnecessary scratching of the same ground. Such duplication, however, should not be confused with the more justifiable repetitions of inquiries where a dominant objective is to dissuade someone by means of publicity. From this point of view, for example, little fault may be found in the frequent inquiries into conditions so difficult of supervision as is lobbying. Likewise, probes into the prices of gasoline may be warranted as habitually as in 1914,[23] 1922,[24] and 1934[25] if the prices have, in spite of other controls, seemed to be fixed by monopolistic combinations.

The facts unearthed by Congressional committees which point to corruption may require more than mere publicity or remedial legislation. A follow-up by the Department of Justice is sometimes called for.[26] Thus, the evidence of alleged collusive bidding uncovered by the select committee of the Senate probing the air mail and ocean mail contracts [27] was turned over to the Department. In this particular instance, however, there

21 S. Res. 246, 71st Cong., 2d Sess., April 17, 1930.

22 H. Res. 237, 73d Cong., 2d Sess., January 29, 1934.

23 S. Res. 457, 63d Cong., 2d Sess., September 28, 1914.

24 S. Res. 295, 67th Cong., 2d Sess., June 5, 1922.

25 S. Res. 166, 73d Cong., 2d Sess., February 2, 1934.

26 Although the Supreme Court has said "It may be conceded that Congress is without authority to compel disclosures for the purpose of aiding the prosecution of pending suits " (Sinclair v. United States, 279 U. S. 295), no law operates to forbid suits instituted as a result of the revelations of a committee which is constitutionally authorized to investigate.

27 S. Res. 349, 72d Cong., 2d Sess., February 25, 1933.

were pronounced repercussions. The Department of Justice, following a reported two-year investigation by a special assistant to the Attorney General, took no steps toward punitive action. Although no report of the findings was made public, the rumors were that no actual fraud had been found. Meanwhile, suits aggregating about $15,000,000 were brought against the government by the air mail companies whose contracts had been annulled. A substantiation for the rumors came in an announcement by the Attorney General in June 1936 that more than half of the claims had been settled for $601,511.[28]

An interesting tie-up with the Department of Justice as well as the National Labor Relations Board was reflected by the activities of the Senate's civil liberties committee [29] relating to the conditions in Harlan County, Kentucky. A series of hearings by the committee in early May 1937 scrutinized an alleged use of murder, kidnapping, and arson to discourage soft-coal miners from joining labor organizations of their own choosing. The direct outgrowth of these disclosures was an investigation by the Department of Justice which resulted in the indictment of sixty-nine Harlan County defendants including twenty-four executives of coal mines, twenty-one mining operators, and twenty-three law enforcement officers. As a basis for its prosecutions, the government selected the Wagner act guaranteeing the right of self-organization, and also a statute of 1870 which makes it a crime to " conspire to injure, oppress, threaten, or intimidate any citizen in the free exercise or enjoyment of any right or privilege secured to him by the Constitution or laws of the United States ... " A trial of nationwide interest began on May 16, 1938, but two and a half months later it ended with the jury hopelessly deadlocked. That the government's drive against the alleged crimes was to be continued was indicated by the immediate filing of a motion

[28] *Annual Report* of the Attorney General of the United States (1936), p. 82.

[29] S. Res. 266, 74th Cong., 2d Sess., June 6, 1936.

for a new hearing.[30] Moreover, three weeks prior to the close of the trial, the National Labor Relations Board also stepped into the breach. Issuing a cease and desist order to the Harlan Fuel Co., one of the defendants, it found that the company had been guilty of unfair labor practices beginning in January 1937, which included threats against and the forcible exclusion of the organizers of the United Mine Workers of America.

Attention to the results of investigations tends to raise questions as to their costs. How much does Congress spend on its inquiries? Do the results warrant the outlays? Complete information on the cost of investigations is not available. Many of the expenses, obviously, never can be determined. A thoroughly accurate picture of the cost to the taxpayers would include, for instance, such overhead as an apportionment of the salaries of the members of the committees covering the time spent in the hearings. Moreover, a standing committee sometimes receives no special appropriation for conducting a minor inquiry; it must, therefore, take its expenses from its regular funds. And administrative bodies frequently lend time and personnel to investigating committees. Recently, however, the Senate has alloted for " inquiries and investigations " average appropriations of close to $300,000 a year. It is hardly

---

[30] In view of Title 28, sec. 634 of the U. S. Code, the inquiring committees which expect a resulting prosecution by the Justice Department are sometimes faced with the problem of determining whether to summon the persons whose conduct is being investigated. This law specifies that " No testimony given by a witness before either House, or before any committee of either House, or before any joint committee established by a joint or concurrent resolution of the two Houses of Congress, shall be used as evidence in any criminal proceeding against him in any court, except in a prosecution for perjury committed in giving such testimony. But an official paper or record produced by him is not within the said privilege." This proviso was adopted because of U. S. Code, Title 2, sec. 193: " No witness is privileged to refuse to testify to any fact, or to produce any paper, respecting which he shall be examined by either House of Congress, or by any joint committee established by a joint or concurrent resolution of the two Houses of Congress, or by any committee of either House, upon the ground that his testimony to such fact or his production of such paper may tend to disgrace him or otherwise render him infamous."

surprising that the figures for the House have reached considerably less than half of this amount. It seems fair to say, nevertheless, that, viewed merely from a dollars and cents angle, the balance sheet of investigations probably would show a profit. This situation is brought about mainly by a further important result of some inquiries. The information which is uncovered frequently enables the Treasury Department to collect additional income taxes. For example, in 1937 the chairman of the committee that inquired into bondholders' committees indicated that " nearly $20,000,000 of income tax has been collected from these committees, receivers, and lawyers where no reports had been made. It was due to our investigation that this money was collected . . . " [31] And the committee investigating stock exchanges and banking stated in its final report: " to date, assessments for deficiencies and penalties have been levied by the Bureau of Internal Revenue in a sum exceeding $2,000,000 as a direct result of the revelations before the subcommittee." [32] These two claims alone would far more than cover the direct outlays in behalf of all the investigations of the past decade.[33]

Whatever other results may flow from Congressional inquiries, a sound investigatory procedure would seem to require that every investigation should at least produce a report by the committee. Yet this document is not always considered essential. An inducement for the omission comes, in some cases, from the resolution of authorization itself. The occasional practice of placing no time limit on investigating committees, for instance, is definitely inadvisable. The Senate's special silver

[31] *Congressional Record*, 75th Cong., 1st Sess., p. 8561, August 9, 1937; the claim was partially supported by a statement from the Bureau of Internal Revenue, p. 8564.

[32] S. Rept. 1455, 73d Cong., 2d Sess., June 16, 1934.

[33] With reference to the Teapot Dome inquiries, a report of the Secretary of the Treasury showed that the additional payments of taxes as a result of the disclosures by the Senate Committee on Public Lands and Surveys, and the investigations by the Treasury Department, totalled $2,005,007 (S. Rept. 157, 70th Cong., 1st Sess., May 28, 1928).

committee [34] was thus "authorized to hold . . . hearings, to sit and act . . . during the sessions and recesses of the Senate in the seventy-fourth and succeeding Congresses . . ." Too often the instructions specify the submission of reports only "as soon as practicable." A few resolutions overlook any mention of either reports or recommendations. The Senate Committee ón Public Lands and Surveys, for example, was ordered to investigate the advisability of establishing additional national parks, and was authorized "to sit, act, and perform its duties at such times and places as it deems necessary or proper . . . ," [35] with no specifications as to a time limit or a report. But even a positive request for a report does not guarantee its delivery; a resolution's mandate is at times simply ignored. Little can be said in defense of such inaction. It may be granted that a turn of circumstances may make an investigation undesirable, or that the probing may reach dead ends, but a report to that effect should be issued. Thus, the House Committee on Labor, which was ordered to study a national old-age pension system, [36] reported its conclusion that "it was not possible to complete its study . . . in time for any action to be had this session." [37] The committees sometimes seem to assume that the mere endorsement of a bill will serve in lieu of a formal report. But more is required. Fellow members of Congress as well as the public deserve a full explanation of the findings and of the bases for the conclusions.

Examples are readily available of committees who failed to issue reports. Four, chosen at random, were: the Senate Banking and Currency Committee inquiring into the operations of the Federal Reserve system; [38] the House Appropriations Committee investigating the eradication of the Mediterranean fruit

[34] S. Res. 187, 74th Cong., 1st Sess., August 16, 1935.

[35] S. Res. 102, 74th Cong., 1st Sess., July 30, 1935.

[36] H. Res. 249, 73d Cong., 2d Sess., February 15, 1934.

[37] H. Rept. 1633, 73d Cong., 2d Sess., May 15, 1934.

[38] S. Res. 71, 71st Cong., 2d Sess., May 5, 1930.

fly;[39] the Senate Finance Committee studying the current economic problems of the United States;[40] and the committee of the Senate probing lobbying in 1935.[41]

It may well be that a committee has no recommendations to make as to legislation. For example, the investigators may seek, by exposure rather than by the enactment of a statute, to prevent certain activities. Regardless of the legislative intent, however, sound procedure would seem to call for a report of the committee's activities. Thus, it is conceivable that the committee's knowledge that a report is required may have the effect of promoting a more orderly inquiry than if no formal accounting is demanded. Moreover, a report, although it may in some instances appear to be of only limited value, may at least help to counteract unjustified criticism of an investigation. It is undeniable that a number of investigations show almost no worthwhile results. The ill-defined intentions of the investigators and the procedural defects already treated contribute to the fruitlessness. The critics, however, sometimes exaggerate their charges of the uselessness of the inquiries; the omission of a report by an investigating committee only helps to sustain this ridicule.

[39] H. Res. 139, 71st Cong., 2d Sess., February 10, 1930.
[40] S. Res. 315, 72d Cong., 2d Sess., January 26, 1933.
[41] S. Res. 165, 74th Cong., 1st Sess., July 11, 1935.

CHAPTER V

RECENT DECISIONS BY THE COURTS

FROM the very beginnings of American government, both houses of Congress have repeatedly obtained information by means of investigating committees. The courts have, however, been slow in providing a clear definition of the scope of the power. The litigation with respect to the Congressional investigative power revolves around two general questions: (1) for what purposes may investigations be conducted; and (2) what are the legal limitations on the activities of the committees who pursue the investigations? Moreover, since the power of inquiry may be aided or hindered by a strengthening or a weakening of the Congressional power to punish for the contempt of one of its committees, a closely related question is: (3) what is the nature of the power of the House or Senate to punish for contempt?

During the past decade several judicial opinions, some of them by the Supreme Court, have thrown a few additional rays of light on each of these questions.

JUDICIAL OPINIONS RELATING TO THE PURPOSES OF INVESTIGATIONS. It may bear repeating that the principal functions of a legislative assembly may be grouped into four classes: to enact laws, to hold the executive officers to a strict accountability, to serve as an organ of public opinion, and to perform certain duties which relate to its own members.[1] It has been seen also that each house of Congress has frequently made use of Congressional investigations in the performance of each of these primary responsibilities. Although the judicial opinions in recent years have been distinctly favorable to Congressional investigating, however, the courts have not yet found occasion to declare specifically that all four of the major purposes of the inquiries are valid.

[1] See *supra*, p. 23.

Prior to the period of this study, the Supreme Court handed down three important decisions relative to the purposes for which Congress may conduct investigations. In the case of Kilbourn v. Thompson [2] in 1881 the court found little ground for the contention that there existed a power to inquire and commit for contempt " to enable either House of Congress to exercise successfully their function of legislation." But Mr. Justice Miller did not venture a decisive statement: " This latter proposition is one which we do not propose to decide in the present case, because we are able to decide it without passing upon the existence or non-existence of such a power in aid of the legislative function." In discussing the power of inquiry, however, the court admitted that the House could fine or imprison a contumacious witness where his examination was necessary to the exercise of the constitutional power of judging the elections and qualifications of its members. Justice Miller also recognized a power to inquire in connection with the impeachment process: " The House of Representatives has the sole right to impeach officers of the government, and the Senate to try them. Where the question of such impeachment is before either body acting in its appropriate sphere on that subject, we see no reason to doubt the right to compel the attendance of witnesses, and their answer to proper questions, in the same manner and by the use of the same means that courts of justice can in like cases." The dictum of the Kilbourn case therefore upheld a power of investigation in two limited areas.

In the case of In re Chapman [3] in 1897 a third field of inquiry was declared to be valid. The court in its decision upheld the Senate's power to investigate, by means of a committee, the conduct of its members. A resolution had authorized an inquiry into the lobbying activities of the " sugar trust " on the tariff act of 1894. The contumacy of Chapman, a New York broker, resulted when the committee probed an alleged speculation in sugar stocks by some Senators. The court main-

[2] 103 U. S. 168.
[3] 166 U. S. 661.

tained that since the inquiry might lead to censure or expulsion, which were legitimate functions of the Senate, it was valid.

A broad expansion of Congress's power to investigate came in the case of McGrain v. Daugherty [4] in 1927. The Supreme Court, for the first time, approved investigations conducted for the purpose of helping Congress to legislate. The Senate or House, declared Mr. Justice Van Devanter, "has power, through its own processes, to compel a private individual to appear before it or one of its committees and give testimony needed to enable it efficiently to exercise a legislative function belonging to it under the Constitution . . . This power is so far incidental to the legislative function as to be implied." The subject of the investigation in this instance was, said the court, "the administration of the Department of Justice . . . Plainly (a subject) on which legislation could be had." Although the resolution contained no express avowal of a legislative intent, the justices agreed that this was not indispensable.

The Supreme Court's decisions of the past decade have added little to the law as to what constitute the valid purposes for which Congress may investigate. It would appear, however, that the opinion in Sinclair v. United States,[5] decided in April 1929, brought a slight broadening of the field of investigation. Like McGrain v. Daugherty, the case stemmed from the Teapot Dome scandals. The Secretaries of the Navy and Interior, by the authority of an act of 1920, had leased public lands containing oil to the Mammoth Oil Company. The president and sole stockholder of the corporation was Harry F. Sinclair. The charges of fraud and bad faith in the making of this and another contract induced the authorization by the Senate of an investigation: "the Committee on Public Lands and Surveys be authorized to investigate this entire subject of leases upon naval oil reserves with particular reference to the protection of the rights and equities of the Government of the

[4] 273 U. S. 135.
[5] 279 U. S. 263.

United States and the preservation of its natural resources, and to report its findings and recommendation to the Senate." [6] A later amendment granted the power of subpoena to the committee.[7] Beginning December 4, 1923, Sinclair testified before the committee on five occasions. By early February sufficient evidence of corruption had been revealed to warrant the adoption of a joint resolution declaring the leases to be against the public interest, and directing the President not only to cause suit to be instituted for their annulment but also " to prosecute such other actions or proceedings, civil and criminal, as may be warranted by the facts." [8] Sinclair, summoned a sixth time, was asked by Senator Walsh on March 22, 1924: " Mr. Sinclair, I desire to interrogate you about a matter concerning which the committee had no knowledge or reliable information at any time when you had heretofore appeared before the committee and with respect to which you must then have had knowledge. I refer to the testimony given by Mr. Bonfils concerning a contract that you made with him touching the Teapot Dome. I wish you would tell us about that." [9] The witness, refusing to answer, called the attention of the committee to a suit already commenced against the Mammoth Oil Co. and maintained that the Senate, by the enactment of the joint resolution, had exhausted its power. The matter had, he insisted, been made a judicial question determinable only in the courts : " I shall reserve any evidence I may be able to give for those courts to which you and your colleagues have deliberately referred all questions of which you had any jurisdiction and shall respectfully decline to answer any questions propounded by your committee." On the recommendation of the

6 S. Res. 282, 67th Cong., 2d Sess., April 29, 1922.

7 S. Res. 294, 67th Cong., 2d Sess., June 5, 1922.

8 43 Stat. 5, February 8, 1924.

9 *Leases Upon Naval Oil Reserves*, Hearings before the Committee on Public Lands and Surveys, pursuant to S. Res. 147, 68th Cong., p. 2897. The contract provided for the payment of $250,000 by the Mammoth Oil Co. to F. G. Bonfils and J. L. Stack for the relinquishment of their rights to leased public lands.

Committee on Public Lands and Surveys, the Senate directed
its President to certify to the district attorney for the District
of Columbia the facts as reported by the commitee. Sinclair,
indicted by a grand jury on March 31, was tried in the Supreme
Court of the District which found him guilty of violating
section 102 of the Revised Statutes.[10] Sentenced to a fine of
five hundred dollars and three months in jail, Sinclair appealed
and the Court of Appeals of the District of Columbia certified
the questions of law to the United States Supreme Court. The
latter chose to consider the entire record and to pass on all the
phases of the appeal, rather than to answer the specific questions. The appellant contended that the interrogations which
he refused to answer " related to his private affairs and to
matters cognizable only in the courts," and maintained that
the committee had departed from any investigation in the aid
of legislation. The court, refusing to accept Sinclair's con-
tentions, affirmed his conviction.

The most significant assertions in the opinion were those
which seemed to broaden slightly the purposes for which
Congress may inquire. After affirming Congress's constitutional power to dispose of and make all the needful rules and
regulations respecting the oil reserves, the court added: "And
undoubtedly the Senate had power to delegate authority to its
committee to investigate and report what had been and was
being done by executive departments under the Leasing Act,
the Naval Oil Reserve Act, and the President's order in respect of the reserves, and to make any other inquiry concerning

[10] Same as U. S. Code, Title 2, sec. 192. First enacted in 1857, the law
has been amended, most recently by 52 Stat. 942, June 13, 1938. The statute
provides: "Every person who having been summoned as a witness by the
authority of either House of Congress, to give testimony or to produce papers
upon any matter under inquiry before either House, or any joint committee
established by a joint or concurrent resolution of the two Houses of Congress,
or any committee of either House of Congress, wilfully makes default, or
who, having appeared, refuses to answer any question pertinent to the question
under inquiry, shall be deemed guilty of a misdemeanor, punishable by a fine
of not more than $1,000 nor less than $100, and imprisonment in a common
jail for not less than one month nor more than twelve months."

the public domain . . . Congress, in addition to its general legislative power over the public domain, had all the powers of a proprietor and was authorized to deal with it as a private individual may deal with lands owned by him. The committee's authority to investigate extended to matters affecting the interest of the United States as owner as well as to those having relation to the legislative function . . . Moreover, it was pertinent for the Senate to ascertain the practical effect of recent changes that had been made in the laws relating to oil and other mineral lands in the public domain." While in McGrain v. Daugherty it had been held that Congress may conduct an investigation for the purpose of enabling it to exercise a legislative function, and the court had agreed that the administration of the law is a legitimate subject of inquiry, the decision in that case did not specifically declare that the Senate or House may investigate as to the effects of the laws which it enacts. It may be argued that this right can be implied from the Daugherty case, but the uncertainty on that point is sufficient to warrant the conclusion that the Sinclair decision not only reinforced the Congressional power to investigate but also, by directly asserting that Congress may inquire as to the effects of its laws, broadened the power to some extent.[11] The expansion was, however, on the basis of the potentiality of the enactment of legislation in the future.

In three other cases of recent years, the Supreme Court settled two questions as to the validity of the purposes of Congressional investigations. In spite of the dictum in Kilbourn v. Thompson, some doubts had continued to exist as to the authority of Congress to investigate pursuant to its duty of judging " the elections, returns and qualifications " of its members. Any uncertainties were erased, however, by the decision in Reed v. The County Commissioners of Delaware County, Pennsylvania,[12] a case involving a special Senate com-

[11] Charles W. Shull, "Congressional Investigations and Contempts," 63 United States Law Review 326 (1929).

[12] 277 U. S. 376 (1928).

mittee which had been created [13] to investigate the methods
employed to influence the nomination of candidates for the
Senate.[14] The previous dictum was affirmed when the court
asserted that the constitutional power of the Senate to judge
the qualifications of its members " carries with it authority
to take such steps as may be appropriate and necessary to
secure information upon which to decide concerning elections."
Moreover, in Barry v. United States,[15] a case which concerned
the same committee of the Senate, the Supreme Court reiterated
the conclusion which it had expressed in the Reed case that the
inquiry was within the constitutional authority of the Senate.[16]
And in the most recent of the Supreme Court's cases concerning Congressional committees of inquiry, United States v.
Norris,[17] the decision clearly demonstrated to the doubters
that the field of inquiry may include primaries as well
as " elections ".[18]

[13] S. Res. 195, 69th Cong., 1st Sess., May 19, 1926.

[14] The controversy arose when a representative of the committee was
directed to take possession of a quantity of ballots in Delaware County, Pennsylvania, and the election officials refused to surrender them. When the
committee and its agent brought suit to obtain the ballots, the court held that
the committee did not have the authority to sue.

[15] 279 U. S. 597 (1929).

[16] The litigation resulted when Thomas Cunningham, an $8,000 a year
clerk of a court, refused to divulge to the committee any information as to
the source of $50,000 which he had given to an organization supporting
William S. Vare for Senator from Pennsylvania. When a warrant was
issued ordering Cunningham to appear before the bar of the Senate to
answer questions which were pertinent to the inquiry, he brought habeas
corpus proceedings. The District Court, discharging the writ, was upheld
by the Supreme Court.

[17] 300 U. S. 564 (1937).

[18] The case involved a question broader than the investigative power.
Norris had testified before a Senate committee investigating campaign expenditures, but, after hearing the statements of another witness, had obtained
the permission of the committee to return to the stand, and had admitted
that some of his testimony had been false. He was indicted for perjury and
convicted in a District Court. Following a reversal of the decision by the
Circuit tribunal, the Supreme Court granted a writ of certiorari. The court
held for the first time that in federal criminal law " retraction (does not)

In summary, then, the Supreme Court has specifically avowed the power of a house of Congress to conduct two classes of investigations—those which have been characterized as membership and those which assist Congress in legislating; moreover, the court has also approved, on the basis that legislation possibly may result, those inquiries which have been termed supervisory. There remains, however, an unsettled question concerning the supervisory inquiries—how far can Congress go in obtaining information from the executive branch of the government? Does the separation of powers of the federal government protect the executive officers, in the final analysis, from unwanted scrutiny by a legislative committee? Or, does the legislature, in the pursuance of the duty which is generally accredited to it of supervising the Executive, possess the authority to require the testimony of and the production of papers by administrators? In the past decade, the executive officers have acquiesced to the requests of the investigating committees for facts. Since an administrator usually runs the risk of creating a suspicion on the part of Congress and of the public if he does not comply with a demand for information, and since Congress, by its control over appropriations, can exert strong pressure on an administrator to submit facts, the Senate and House generally obtain the information which they want. The committees of earlier years did, on occasion, encounter refusals by administrators to supply

neutralize false testimony previously given and exculpate the witness of perjury." As applied to Congressional investigating, the case serves to reinforce the power of a committee to obtain information. The committees are protected from deliberately false testimony offered by a witness who may, if discovered, purge himself by substituting the truth.

A Circuit Court of Appeals had, in 1935, rendered a decision, Seymour v. United States, 77 F (2d) 577, which closely paralleled the later Norris opinion. The Seymour case resulted when another witness committed perjury before the same Senate committee that was involved in the Norris case. The Circuit Court supported the authority of Congress to investigate primaries and took the position that "if false material testimony was knowingly given, perjury had been committed and nothing thereafter done could alter that situation."

information.[19] But, because both the Senate and the House eventually retreated upon the flat refusal of the executives to answer questions, the legal problems which are involved were never presented to the courts.[20] Thus, it remains an open

[19] See Dimock, *op. cit.*, p. 106, for a reference to a conflict between President Andrew Jackson and an investigating committee of the House.

[20] Although no executive officers refused to submit information to any investigating committee during the period of this study, a few examples may be cited of conflicts in connection with another Congressional technique of gathering information — resolutions of inquiry (see *supra*, p. 10). In each of these instances the Senate or House failed to obtain the information which it requested.

When the House in 1932 requested all the documents pertaining to an investigation, by the Treasury Department, of the importation of ammonium sulphate (H. Res. 213, 72d Cong., 1st Sess.), the resolution included the clause "if not incompatible with the public interest." Ogden Mills, the Secretary of the Treasury, felt justified in withholding the papers and explained his position in a letter to the Speaker: "It has been the practice of the department in acting under this statute to treat all information furnished by interested persons as confidential and not to disclose it unless such persons consent to the disclosure. . . . As consent has not been given to the disclosure of the information contained in the record before the Treasury Department, I am of the opinion that it would be incompatible with the public interest to comply with the request contained in the resolution" (*Congressional Record*, 72d Cong., 1st Sess., p. 11669). The letter was received by the House without comment.

Both Mr. Hoover and Mr. Roosevelt, in at least one instance each, deemed it unwise to comply with resolutions of inquiry. The Roosevelt incident was of only minor importance, and his refusal to supply the information went unchallenged. A resolution (H. Res. 212, 74th Cong., 1st Sess.) of the House in 1935 requested the President to transmit the full text of one of his press conferences. The President considered it inadvisable, however, "to create the precedent of sending to the Congress for documentary use the text of remarks I make at the bi-weekly conferences with the newspaper representatives" (*Congressional Record*, 74th Cong., 1st Sess., p. 7186). The Senate's conflict with President Hoover, however, concerned a subject of major importance, and the legislative retreat was not made without a strong protest. The Senate's Committee on Foreign Relations, which was studying the London Naval Treaty of 1930, requested from the Secretary of State the papers relating to the negotiations prior to and during the London conference. Some of the documents were submitted, but Secretary Stimson explained that he had been "directed by the President to say" that the production of the others "would not in his opinion be compatible with the public interest." The Foreign Relations Committee, apparently incensed,

question whether the executive officers must submit all the information which Congress may request. It may be argued, however, that if impeachment charges are pending, Congress has no authority to compel testimony by an official for the purpose of aiding his prosecution, since such coercion would constitute self-incrimination.[21]

The remaining purpose for which investigations are conducted, to assist Congress in its task of informing the public, has not been judicially approved. Although no federal court, in discussing the bases for the Congressional power of investigation, has yet recognized this informing function of a legislature, it is conceivable that the mere dissemination of information by a committee may in the future become valid grounds

pressed its right "to have free and full access" to the papers and, by the adoption of a resolution, asserted its opinion that the documents were "relevant and pertinent when the Senate is considering a treaty for the purpose of ratification" (*Congressional Record*, 71st Cong., 2d Sess., p. 12030). The resolution drew from Secretary Stimson, however, only a short note reiterating his previous stand. Congress adjourned early in July 1930, but the President immediately called back the Senate to consider the treaty. Only three days of the special session had elapsed when the Senate, backing its Committee on Foreign Relations, adopted, 53 to 4, a resolution requesting the President, "if not incompatible with the public interest," to submit to the Senate "with such recommendations as he may make respecting their use" all the documents concerning the negotiation of the treaty (S. Res. 320, 71st Cong., Special session of the Senate). A Presidential reply, received the next day, pleaded the confidential character of the papers, and expressed the assurance that "the Senate does not wish me to commit such a breach of trust" (S. Doc. 216, 71st Cong., Special session of the Senate). The Senate was by no means satisfied, but it avoided any further wrangling. Senatorial face was saved by a resolution proposed by Senator Norris; consent was given to the ratification of the treaty, but with "the distinct and explicit understanding" that there were no secret papers or agreements tending to modify or define its terms (*Congressional Record*, 71st Cong., Special session of the Senate, p. 362, July 21, 1930).

[21] See Charles W. Shull, "Congressional Investigations and Contempts," 63 *United States Law Review* 326 (1929). Also see the Sinclair case at p. 295: "It may be conceded that Congress is without authority to compel disclosures for the purpose of aiding the prosecution of pending suits." No cases have been found which would indicate that the investigatory powers of a committee inquiring as to charges of impeachment are any greater or any less than those of committees probing other subjects.

for an inquiry.[22] Whether or not this development occurs, however, may be of little practical consequence to the Congressional
investigators, since the courts seem to be leaning in the direction of conceding that an investigation has a legislative purpose,
even though the aim be indistinct; a statement of such purpose
in the authorizing resolution is generally sufficient to convince
the court that it exists. This current disposition of the courts

[22] A slight move in this direction may be indicated by a District Court's
decision sustaining the power of the Railroad Labor Board to compel testimony: "It does not follow that, because the decision of the board . . . is
merely published in order to guide public opinion, the proceedings in court
to compel evidence upon which to base the finding of the board are advisory.
. . . If resort may not be had to the courts to assist administrative bodies
to obtain evidence in matters under investigation by them, even though those
investigations do not lead to an order enforceable in the courts, it would be
impossible to perform its functions under the Constitution. . . . The Labor
Board is charged with the duty . . . of rendering decisions concerning dis-
putes between carriers and their employees. While the decision . . . is not
enforceable by process, it does have behind it the force of public opinion.
'The function of the Labor Board is to direct public criticism against the
party, who, it thinks, justly deserves it'". This decision, Railroad Labor
Board v. Robertson, 3 F (2d) 488 (1925), was reversed (268 U. S. 619),
although on other grounds. See Theodore W. Cousens, "The Purposes and
Scope of Investigations under Legislative Authority," 26 Georgetown Law
Journal 905 (1938).
   It is also interesting to note the Supreme Court's position in Standard
Computing Scale Co. v. Farrell, 249 U. S. 571 (1919), that the dissemination of information by the New York State Superintendent of
Weights and Measures was not in the range of governmental action. The
controversy in this case arose when the Superintendent, after "prolonged
investigation and extensive experimentation," issued, in a "bulletin of in-
struction and information" for dealers and for "weights and measures
officials," a "specification" that "all combination spring and lever computing
scales must be equipped with a device which will automatically compensate
for changes of temperature." Because of this "specification", some county
and city sealers of weights "neglected to seal scales of plaintiff's make and
warned scale users to discontinue the use thereof"; and a state inspector
also marked some of these scales "slow and faulty." The Standard Co.
contended that the "specification" was arbitrary and unreasonable, that it
was discriminatory, and that it interfered with interstate commerce. The
court, however, dismissed the bill on the grounds that the "specification"
was "not in the nature of a law or regulation," but "educational" and
"advisory", and that, therefore, "the prohibitions of the Federal Constitution cannot apply."

to find that Congress is investigating for the purpose of determining whether any legislation is desirable, permits inquiry in a vast area. The principal effect, therefore, of the judiciary's explicit approval of the investigations which are calculated to disseminate information would probably be only to remove the necessity for disguising a purely informing probe as one with law-making aims.

LEGAL LIMITATIONS ON THE ACTIVITIES OF INVESTIGATING COMMITTEES.   Although there seem to be few restrictions on the subjects into which Congressional committees can inquire, the constitutional rights of individuals, as guaranteed in the fourth and fifth amendments, serve as a definite check on the methods which the committees may employ. Thus, it has been held that neither house of Congress has any " general " power to search into, or compel disclosures concerning, private affairs. The courts, therefore, may be called upon to judge the legality of the subpoenas which a committee issues. The judiciary has likewise asserted its authority to review the activities of the committees in order to ascertain if the questions propounded in the hearings are pertinent to the matter under inquiry. In actual practice the courts are liberal in construing the meaning of the law and appear to be reluctant to refuse to sustain the committees. The one important restriction on an investigating committee during the period of this study, Strawn v. Western Union Telegraph Company, served to emphasize, however, that the compulsory powers of Congressional committees are limited by the private rights guaranteed in the fourth amendment. The committee of the Senate which began investigating lobbying in 1935 [23] had issued a subpoena ordering from the Western Union Company the copies of all the telegrams which had been sent or received by the Chicago law firm of Winston, Strawn, and Shaw between February 1 and December 1, 1935. A petition by Silas H. Strawn for a permanent injunction, to enjoin Western Union from delivering the telegrams, was

[23] S. Res. 165, 74th Cong., 1st Sess., July 11, 1935.

heard in the Supreme Court of the District of Columbia.[24] Chief Justice Wheat, after listening to the arguments for both sides, suddenly halted the rebuttal of the counsel for Strawn. " Mr. Hogan," he interrupted, " I do not believe that I want to hear any more. I have listened to the case very fully. It has been fairly argued on both sides. It does not make any difference whether it is Mr. Silas Strawn or who it is." Whereupon he launched into a criticism of the subpoena. Insisting that he " would be the last one in the world to claim any right to interfere with the powers of the Senate or with its legitimate discretion," he nevertheless felt bound to grant the injunction: " That is the view I take of it, that this subpoena goes way beyond the legitimate use of the subpoena *duces tecum*,[25] and that

[24] 3 *United States Law Week* 646; and *New York Times*, March 12, 1936.

[25] The court's position in this case does not appear to be unreasonable. It would seem that some attempt should have been made by the committee to describe particularly the telegrams which it sought. Nevertheless, something can be said for the desirability of the courts' sanction of rather general subpoenas issued by Congressional committees *who have good reason to know that pertinent material will be found.* An excessive insistence on particularity may seriously frustrate an inquiry. The encouragement furnished by the Strawn decision doubtless contributed largely to the later refusal of the representatives of the National Committee to Uphold Constitutional Government to produce documents before the same Senate committee. Thus, one subpoena called for a " record " showing the names of all the persons who had contributed one hundred dollars or more to the organization, together with the dates and the amounts of the contributions. But the counsel for the National Committee maintained that " if there were such a record, unless the committee can particularize and describe it more fully, with the names of the contributors and the dates of the contributions in full, the committee (National Committee to Uphold Constitutional Government) does not feel it should produce that material. So I am advising you that this subpoena will not be complied with " (Hearings, p. 2146). That Congressional committees should be required to describe in too great detail the papers which they seek, would, on occasion, probably forestall desirable legislative investigating. Moreover, the Supreme Court has at times upheld extremely broad subpoenas for papers, although they were issued by federal grand juries. See 36 *Columbia Law Review* 842 (1936).

This defiance on the part of the attorney for the National Committee to Uphold Constitutional Government, it should be noted, was successful. Indeed, the conclusion is not justified that all or even most of the contumacious witnesses before the investigating committees become subjects of punitive

the plaintiffs here have a legitimate interest in the controversy, and they have the right to be protected by the court when they claim protection under the Fourth Amendment to the Constitution." [26]

or coercive activities by the House or Senate. In reality, the majority of the instances of a refusal to testify, or to produce subpoenaed papers, pass without a serious challenge. Ordinarily, a recusant witness becomes the signal for an executive session by the committee concerned, where a vote is taken on the procedure to be followed. More often than not, the point will not be pressed. This decision may result from the committee's doubts as to its own legal rights—a question which is propounded extemporaneously, for instance, may on reflection appear to overstep valid bounds. More likely, however, the members of the committee will consider the possession of the desired information, whether or not it is available from another source, as hardly worth the effort of any additional formal proceedings. A warrant to bring a witness before the bar of the House or Senate can be issued only after a majority vote of approval of the chamber concerned. Or, if an indictment and a court trial are sought, the same majority vote is required plus, perhaps, a grant of funds for the hire of counsel to fight the case. Although such an approval may not be difficult to obtain, the members of a committee must almost certainly spend time in arranging for a favorable reception to their resolution. Celebrated examples of challenges to the powers of two Senate investigating committees were the successful defiances by Bishop James Cannon and other leaders of the "Anti-Smith Democrats" of 1928. See Clarence Cannon, *op. cit.*, pp. 168-176; also S. Rept. 43, 71st Cong., 2d Sess., part 10, and S. Rept. 24, 72d Cong., 1st Sess.

[26] In the same month in which the Strawn decision was delivered, W. R. Hearst brought suit to enjoin the same committee and the Federal Communications Commission from copying and using the telegraph offices' transcripts of the wires sent by him to his employees. A subpoena *duces tecum* of the committee had allegedly demanded the delivery of all the communications transmitted through the Washington telegraph offices between February 1 and September 1, 1935. The Hearst bill charged that the reluctance of the telegraph companies to produce the wires led the committee to seek assistance from the Federal Communications Commission, and that the committee and the Commission (the Commission urged its interest due to the alleged forging of telegrams and to the burning of file copies, S. Doc. 188, 74th Cong., 2d Sess.) "conspired together to deprive appellant of his constitutional rights and liberties." Mr. Hearst's action, therefore, was an attempt to dissolve a novel relationship between a legislative committee and a regulatory commission. Chief Justice Wheat, of the Supreme Court of the District of Columbia, arguing a lack of jurisdiction, dismissed the application for the injunction to restrain the committee's use of the telegrams, but claimed

CONGRESSIONAL POWER TO PUNISH FOR CONTEMPT. One of the two or three most significant decisions relating to investigations in the past decade was delivered in the case of Jurney v. MacCracken.[27] In it the Supreme Court had an opportunity to clarify the nature of the power of the Senate or the House to punish for the contempt of a committee. The previous judicial pronouncements seemed to warrant the assumption that this power could be exercised only as " a means to legislative information." [28] One observer, for example, had declared it to be " really not a punitive power at all; it is a coercive power." [29] The opinion of Jurney v. MacCracken, however, tended to broaden the scope of the power.

A Senate resolution of the seventy-second Congress had directed a select committee to investigate the existing air mail and ocean mail contracts concluded between the Postmaster General and the private operators.[30] In the course of the hearings, William P. MacCracken, Jr., a Washington lawyer, was served with a subpoena *duces tecum* which requested him to appear before the committee and to bring all books of account

"a perfect right" to enjoin the Commission from proceeding unlawfully. The immediate issue was not faced, however, since the Commission had informed the court that its investigation was completed and that it had no copies of Hearst's telegrams in its possession. The injunction was therefore denied "without prejudice to its renewal upon any evidence of further activities along the lines attacked here." On the appeal to the United States Court of Appeals for the District of Columbia the decree of the lower tribunal was affirmed, Hearst v. Black, 87 F (2d) 68 (1936). Justice Groner, speaking for the court, approved the refusal of a stay of the Federal Communications Commission, but agreed that the Commission's help to the committee had been unlawful and that its seizure of the wires should have been enjoined if the bill had been filed "while the trespass was in process." Answering the appellant's prayer that the committee on lobbying be prohibited from using the telegrams, he insisted that in spite of the unlawful procurement of the information, the court could not dictate as to its use or non-use by the committee.

[27] 294 U. S. 125 (1935).

[28] Dimock, *op. cit.*, p. 148.

[29] Eberling, *op. cit.*, p. 318. See Marshall v. Gordon, 243 U. S. 521 (1917).

[30] S. Res. 349, 72d Cong., 2d Sess., February 25, 1933.

and papers "relating to air mail and ocean mail contracts." The witness presented himself as requested, but claimed client immunity for much of the correspondence between himself and the corporations or individuals for whom he had acted as attorney. On the committee's suggestion, he at once wired his clients asking if they wished to waive the privilege. Affirmative replies were immediately received from most of the clients, and on February 1, 1934 MacCracken produced all the papers relating to the business of the firms consenting to the waiver. Before MacCracken had received an answer from Western Air Express, Inc., however, a Mr. Givvin of that company, on orders from his superior, Mr. Hanshue, went to Mac-Cracken's office and, with the consent of MacCracken, withdrew several letters (all allegedly, but not actually, personal) from the files. Similarly, Mr. Brittin, vice-president of Northwest Airways, after gaining the permission not of MacCracken but of MacCracken's partner, examined his company's files in the lawyers' office and removed some papers. The Brittin letters, which were asserted to be strictly personal and unrelated to the subject matter of the investigation, were torn and thrown in a wastepaper basket. By the afternoon of February 2, Mac-Cracken had received waivers from all his clients and promptly produced all the papers then remaining in his files. The next day, Givvin returned the letters which he had removed. "Most" of Brittin's letters also came into the hands of the committee by the aid of inspectors of the Post Office Department, who searched through waste and were able to paste the torn bits together in their original form. A Senate resolution was then enacted citing MacCracken, Brittin, Givvin, and Hanshue for contempt of the Senate.[31] Brought before the bar of the Senate, Givvin and Hanshue were found not guilty. Brittin, however, was adjudged guilty and was sentenced to ten days in jail. MacCracken, declining to appear in response to the citation, also was found guilty of contempt of the Senate, but was released on a $5,000 bond pending appeal. A petition for a writ of

[31] S. Res. 172, 73d Cong., 2d Sess., February 5, 1934.

habeas corpus against the Senate's sergeant-at-arms was dismissed by the Supreme Court of the District of Columbia, but the Court of Appeals reversed the judgment.[32] The respondent did not question the constitutional power of the Senate to make the investigation, nor the validity of the subpoena *duces tecum.* His main contention was " that the Senate was without power to arrest him with a view to punishing him, because the act complained of — the alleged destruction and removal of the papers after service of the subpoena—was ' the past commission of a completed act which prior to the arrest and the proceedings to punish had reached such a stage of finality that it could no longer affect the proceedings of the Senate or any Committee thereof, and which, and the effects of which, had been undone long before the arrest '."

The case was of considerable import to investigating committees. Had an unfavorable conclusion been reached and the Senate and House been denied the power to punish a witness who destroyed papers after the service of a subpoena, disturbing hindrances to investigations would have been fostered. A realization of the possible implications to Congress of an adverse opinion probably induced Hatton W. Sumners, the chairman of the House committee on the Judiciary, to argue the case as amicus curiae.

Mr. Justice Brandeis, speaking for a unanimous court,[33] admitted the limits of the power of the houses of Congress to punish for contempt and asserted that " No act is so punishable unless it is of a nature to obstruct the performance of the duties of the legislature." But he gave a broad interpretation to the verb " obstruct ": " Where the offending act was of a nature to obstruct the legislative process, the fact that the obstruction has since been removed, or that its removal has become impossible is without legal significance." Whether MacCracken was guilty, therefore, and " whether he has so far purged himself of contempt that he does not now deserve pun-

[32] 72 F (2d) 560.

[33] Mr. Justice McReynolds took no part in the consideration or decision.

ishment," were declared to be questions for the Senate to decide. " The respondent to the petition," insisted the court, " did not, by demurring, transfer to the court the decision of these questions." The opinion, therefore, by expanding the legitimate scope of the Congressional power to punish for contempt, in effect strengthened the investigatory power of the Senate and the House.

SUMMARY. The judicial opinions of the past decade have, on the whole, been favorable to the Congressional power of investigation. Almost without exception the courts, when questions have arisen concerning the legality of particular investigations, have sustained the Congressional committees.[34] In so doing, they have tended to broaden slightly the purposes for which the House or Senate may conduct inquiries.

Prior to the period of this study, the Supreme Court, in three cases, had issued opinions as to the validity of the purposes of investigations by Congress. The court had admitted in the dictum of Kilbourn v. Thompson that the House can fine or imprison a contumacious witness where his examination is necessary to the exercise of the power of impeachment or to judging the elections and qualifications of the members of the House; in In re Chapman it had affirmed the power of Congress to inquire concerning the conduct of its members; and in the decision of McGrain v. Daugherty it had held that the power of investigation is an essential corollary of the lawmaking function.

Beginning in 1928 three Supreme Court opinions served to reinforce a part of the dictum of Kilbourn v. Thompson. Reed v. County Commissioners and Barry v. United States affirmed the authority of a house of Congress to inquire into the " elections, returns and qualifications " of its members; and in the succeeding Norris decision the court removed any doubt that

---

[34] The most recent case to go beyond the District Courts, Townsend v. United States, 95 F (2d) 352 (1938), serves to illustrate the courts' continued approval of Congressional investigations. See supra, p. 31.

had continued to exist as to the right of the Senate or House to investigate primaries as well as " elections ".

Sinclair v. United States, perhaps the most important case of the past decade, recognized, as had McGrain v. Daugherty, that " legislative " investigations include those into the administration of the law; but the Sinclair opinion also, for the first time, sanctioned inquiries for the purpose of obtaining information on the practical effects of the laws already passed. Although both the Daugherty and Sinclair decisions attested to the validity of investigations into the administration of the law, in neither case did the court have to determine specifically whether, in view of the separation of powers in the federal government, the power of the committees to conduct these " supervisory " investigations embodies the authority to compel the executive officers themselves to give testimony. Indeed, this issue has never been presented to the courts.

The judiciary has, then, upheld investigations pertaining to three of the main purposes for which they are conducted— law-making, supervisory, and membership. Although no court has stated that the dissemination of information is also a valid purpose for a Congressional inquiry, the practical effect of the decisions is to approve the inquiries of this category. This conclusion may be drawn because of the present proclivity of the courts to find that an investigation is being conducted for the purpose of ascertaining whether any legislation is desirable, even though the aim is indistinct. The restrictions on the scope of the investigative power, in fact, apparently have been so far relaxed as to justify the conclusion that the law as it now stands permits the conduct of inquiries in an area about as wide as the legislators may wish, especially if a legislative intent is expressed in the resolution of authorization.

Moreover, along with the judicial broadening of the purposes for which Congress may investigate has come a strengthening of the power of inquiry as a result of the pronouncement by the Supreme Court in Jurney v. MacCracken that the legislative power to punish for contempt is not confined to purposes of coercion, but may be employed also against past, although removed, obstruction to investigating committees.

Although the legitimate scope of the Congressional power of inquiry is extensive, the persons who are being investigated are protected by the private rights guaranteed to the individual in the bill of rights. While the line between these two conflicting sets of rights is not clearly defined,[35] the judiciary has maintained its authority to call a halt to a committee's activities if they interfere with private rights. Thus, the courts have on occasion reiterated the rule laid down in Kilbourn v. Thompson that neither house of Congress "possesses the general power of making inquiry into the private affairs of the citizen." The one important restriction on an investigating committee during the past decade, which resulted when a lower court, in Strawn v. Western Union, declared that a committee's blanket subpoena *duces tecum* violated the fourth amendment to the constitution, served to remind the investigating committees that their powers are limited. It appears to be incontestable, however, that, on the whole, the present disposition of the courts is to sustain the committees in the controversies which arise; the presumption seems to be in favor of the regularity of a committee's proceedings.

[35] Dimock, *op. cit.*, chap. VI.

CHAPTER VI
CONCERNING FUTURE METHODS

CONGRESSIONAL investigations are useful cogs in the wheels of the American system of government. Each general function of Congress is more effectively performed as a result of the facts which are gleaned by inquiring committees. There are abuses, however. Indeed, so intermingled are the misuses and the benefits of the inquiries that extreme praise of or vituperation against investigations as a whole, if made in good faith, hardly reflects more than a patchwork knowledge of them. More significant than the mere presence of the abuses, however, is the inescapable conclusion that—again speaking generally—little has been accomplished by way of correction in a score of years. The absence of improvement must bring a feeling of discouragement to persons who are interested in efficient governmental processes.

There have been shining examples of investigations of the better type; the Pecora-Fletcher inquiry into the stock exchanges and banking may be cited as only one—its legislative results and its accomplishments in moulding public opinion speak for themselves. Perhaps an equal number of inquiries, however, have injured the prestige of Congressional investigating. These mismanaged investigations — present in each Congress—have an important share in contributing to the ridicule which many inquiries receive from the general public and to which previous writers have referred.[1] It is difficult to judge whether this ridicule has increased or decreased during the past decade. There seems to be little basis, however, for concluding that it has subsided to any appreciable degree. The scoffing is admittedly fostered in part by those persons who are seeking defenses against damaging revelations made by the committees. Moreover, the significance of a particular inquiry may be blurred for the man on the street because the press frequently

---

[1] Dimock, *op. cit.*, p. 170.

features the absurd side of investigations at the expense of the more important but less colorful proceedings. Nevertheless, ridicule is too often justifiable to be dismissed as resulting entirely from misrepresentations by the press or the jibes of injured persons.

What then may be proposed to improve the conduct of investigations? It is scarcely debatable that many and varied inquiries are essential in connection with the legislative functions. But it is more controversial whether the Congressmen themselves should conduct the inquiries. Congress should perhaps turn over more of its investigations to others. Considerable thought in recent years has centered on the advisability of the delegation to the executive of the legislative, or rule-making, power. As the government has entered new fields of endeavor, and as the problems which it must meet have become more complex, the necessity for Congress to shift some of its burden has become increasingly recognized. Let Congress lay down the general policy and let the administrators fill in the details—so runs the argument. An impressive case can also be made for the frequent delegation by Congress of its fact-finding authority. The decision as to what types of agencies should be entrusted with the inquiries involves a separate problem which will be treated presently; at this point it is sufficient to say that the delegation may be made (1) to an *ad hoc* body consisting of government officials or of the public or of both, which is established for the purpose of conducting a specific investigation, or (2) to a permanent governmental agency. A permanent body may, on the one hand, be given instructions by one or both houses of Congress to conduct a particular inquiry. Or it may, on the other hand, have a continuing investigative duty and therefore require no further directions, only appropriations, from Congress.

A compelling reason for the Congressional delegation to others of some investigations is that the legislators simply have too much to do. The repeated absences of the committeemen from the investigations' hearings are indicative of other duties which presumably are more pressing. The situation is of course altered with respect to hearings conducted between sessions. But almost all important inquiries are made, at least in part, while Congress is sitting. If an investigating Senator or Representative spends the long hours necessary for an adequate preparation and understanding of the details,[2] his other legislative duties are likely to suffer. An indication of the demands of an investigation was Senator Wheeler's comment in the midst of the inquiry into railroad financing: " The job is so stupendous that I am frank to say to the Senate that, if I had realized where it was to lead, I probably should not have undertaken it, because it is almost too great a task to be done as it should be done." [3] The law makers must have facts, but this need not imply that the law makers must unearth them.

The case for the frequent delegation of the Congressional power to inquire is also strengthened because much can be said in favor of having the investigators detached from the body which is responsible for the inquiry and for the action resulting from the inquiry. One of the common complaints concerning Congressional investigations arises from the possibility that a committee will combine the roles of prosecutor, jury, and judge. This criticism carries weight. While the system may in most instances produce no injustices, it does furnish a fertile soil for abuse. The Congressmen are bound to carry into investigations their preconceived notions of the truth. To admit this does not in itself point to the advisability of displacing the Senators and Representatives as probers; a completely rigid objectivity can be found in no man. But if a Congressman's ideas as to the truth have impelled him to voice charges and to enlist aid in driving through the Senate or House a resolution of authorization for an inquiry, he may be forced to prove his suppositions to be correct, or suffer serious embarrassment.[4] An impartial

2 See *supra*, p. 59.

3 *Congressional Record*, 75th Cong., 1st Sess., p. 701, February 2, 1937.

4 The sponsor of a resolution, as has been seen, generally conducts the inquiry.

investigation, therefore, is hardly encouraged. It would seem to be a sounder procedure if the inquiries were conducted by persons outside of Congress who would issue comprehensive reports and entrust to other hands any action on their recommendations. Ideally, from the point of view of stimulating the public's confidence in the conclusions, a complete quarantine of one group from the other may be required. While this extreme will not always be wholly practicable, it may be erected as a goal. An illustration, outside the Congressional field, of the possible harmful effects of a failure to maintain this divorce is afforded by President Roosevelt's conferences with his Committee on Administrative Management. Chosen to study and recommend a means of increasing the efficiency in the administration of the federal government,[5] the Committee, prior to the issuance of its conclusions, was reported to have discussed the problems with the President. Since the subject of the inquiry was a responsibility of the Chief Executive and since he had an intimate knowledge of the problems which were involved, Mr. Roosevelt had good reason to consult with the committee. He undoubtedly was able to make valuable suggestions as to the general course of the inquiry. As it turned out, however, it would seem that the President could have adopted a better strategy by insulating himself from the committee until its report was published, at which time he could have expressed his views on the conclusions. Charges of a desire for a " dictatorship " were hurled at the President by his critics when the committee announced its general conviction that " Strong executive leadership is essential to democratic government today." [6] Despite a lack of any evidence of Presidential influence on the final report, the critics were handed a nail on which to hang their opposing arguments.

The ill effects of the publicity which investigations bring to the members of Congress also provide an argument for an

[5] See *supra*, p. 37.

[6] President's Committee on Administrative Management, *Report with Special Studies* (1937), p. 53.

increased delegation of the power to inquire. There is perhaps no swifter escalator to national prominence for a legislator than the direction of an important inquiry. It has been argued, however, that, in general, investigations by Congressional committees should be used only as a last resort,[7] that they should be employed only when other devices are found wanting. If this be conceded, both the Senate and the House have been too prone to sanction inquiries by their own committees. Indeed, duplicate studies are occasionally ratified. Reference has already been made to the overlappings of the Senate and House inquiries into wild-life.[8] A more noted example of duplicate probes resulted in the simultaneous efforts of the lobby investigating committees from both chambers to obtain the testimony of the same witness.[9] While some doubling of legislative activities is to be expected as a consequence of bicameralism, the duplicating inquiries may well be eliminated. It appears reasonable to assume that the ratio of needless investigations would decline in the face of more frequent delegation and the resulting sacrifice by the legislators of the attendant publicity.[10]

[7] Dimock, *op. cit.*, p. 26.

[8] See *supra*, p. 88.

[9] See *supra*, p. 39, footnote. A reception of inquiries was avoided in one instance when the Securities and Exchange Commission in 1934 was ordered to investigate bondholders' reorganizations and protective committees (48 Stat. 881, sec. 211). Although the Commission issued comprehensive questionnaires, none was sent to the real estate committees, since a select group of the House had been directed during the same month to inquire into the real estate reorganization committees (H. Res. 412, 73d Cong., 2d Sess., June 15, 1934). The S. E. C., however, lent personnel to the House committee.

[10] This assumption would seem to be valid whether the delegation is made by one house of Congress or by the two houses jointly. One house, if it entrusts an inquiry to an outside body, can grant no compulsory power to that body. Such power, of course, often is not essential to an investigation. An agency may, however, already possess powers of inquiry which may be used to conduct an investigation requested by the House or Senate alone. Thus, some of the independent regulatory commissions are occasionally asked, by simple resolutions of one house, to make inquiries which require the exercise of the subpoena powers which have been conferred on the commissions by statutes. The actual power of one house to compel a governmental

A further minor drawback to the investigations which are conducted by Congressional committees is their unavoidable susceptibility to interruption following elections. While the bulk of the inquiries are completed in a few months or even weeks, others continue for several years. The substitutions that are made on a committee as a result of the failure of some of its members to be reelected may bring unfortunate delays. The loose ends of dropped strings are not easily collected. Although in recent years chance has not seriously crippled any important committees in this manner, the possibility remains.

And finally, the frequency with which Congressional investigating committees borrow personnel from the administration may also suggest the advisability of the delegation of the power to inquire. The practice has already been treated in detail.[11] The need for assistance from the executive branch has at times been recognized by the inclusion of a mandate in the Senate and House resolutions that administrative personnel should be lent. And the chairman of the committees have, on occasion, urged the positive necessity of help.   But the weakness of this borrowing from a supervisory point of view is evident; Congress can have no complete information concerning, or control over, the total expenses of investigations. The student of government cannot but wonder whether the dependence of the Congressional committees on executive personnel may not be a signpost indicating the desirability of delegating some inquiries to administrative agencies, where an investigating staff, or a nucleus for a staff, may already be assembled.

agency to conduct an inquiry may be questioned when no statute specifically confers that power. No instance has been found, however, of an agency's refusal to make any study asked for by a resolution of either the House or Senate. It should be noted, in this connection, that Congress provided in 1934 " That hereafter no new investigations shall be initiated by the (Federal Trade) Commission as the result of a legislative resolution, except the same be a concurrent resolution of the two Houses of Congress " (48 Stat. 291). To encourage the delegation of investigations, this provision might be rescinded.

11 See *supra*, p. 63.

Two Types of Investigations Suited to Increased Delegation. It would seem, therefore, that more of the inquiries should be conducted by bodies outside of Congress. The choice of the substitute agencies, however, presents a further problem. Because all inquiries by no means follow a set pattern, an investigatory device which is well suited to one study or type of study may be inappropriate for another. It is suggested that, for the purpose of selecting the most suitable agency for conducting a particular inquiry, the investigations may be roughly separated into two categories based on the nature of the information which is sought. Thus, on the one hand, some inquiries may have the purpose of assembling information which, for one reason or another, someone may prefer to conceal. Those investigations which are aimed at uncovering alleged corruption or practices which may be deemed anti-social may, of course, encounter persons who are reluctant to divulge the facts. Even where no wrong-doing has occurred, however, resistance to an inquiry may be offered if the subject matter touches on those affairs of an individual which he considers personal. It sometimes follows, therefore, that if the facts are to be obtained at all, they must be pried loose by an agency which has been given the power to demand the attendance of witnesses and to compel disclosures. It may be that an actual exercise of this compulsory power will not be necessary, that nothing more than the force of public opinion will be needed to draw out the information; but it may nevertheless be desirable that the investigators are fortified with the power. These inquiries, where the investigators should be able, if necessary, to exert strong pressure to obtain information, may be called " inquisitorial " inquiries. The Senate's investigation of the prices of bread, sugar, and meat,[12] and the House committee's examination of the real estate bondholders' reorganization committees [13] fit the classification. Other examples of the inquisitorial probes of recent years were the inquiries into: the owner-

12 S. Res. 374, 71st Cong., 3d Sess., January 16, 1931.
13 H. Res. 412, 73d Cong., 2d Sess., June 15, 1934.

ship of the public utility corporations by holding companies,[14] the stock exchanges and banking,[15] and the " kick-back racket." [16]

A distinction may be made between the " inquisitorial " investigations and those inquiries in which a power to compel disclosures is of much less importance, although in practically all investigations some inquisitorial activities may be undertaken. The latter may be designated as " research " investigations.[17] The " researchers " do not, in general, have to pry the facts from reluctant sources. Indeed, the investigators may be as interested in collecting opinions as in finding the facts on a particular subject. Examples of what may be characterized as research investigations from those conducted within the past decade were the studies of : unemployment insurance systems,[18] the supply of tin,[19] the advisability of establishing an economic council,[20] the conservation of wild-life,[21] the government's competition with private enterprise,[22] and the problems of unemployment and relief.[23]

A number of the Congressional investigations within both these categories might well be entrusted to agencies outside Congress. The selection of the most appropriate alternative agency is, however, not easy. Because a body which is most suitable for an inquisitorial inquiry may differ from that which is appropriate for a research inquiry, the two classifications are considered separately.

[14] H. Res. 59, 72d Cong., 1st Sess., January 19, 1932.

[15] S. Res. 84, 72d Cong., 1st Sess., March 4, 1932.

[16] S. Res. 228, 73d Cong., 2d Sess., May 30, 1934.

[17] It is not meant to imply that no research work is done in the inquisitorial investigations.

[18] S. Res. 483, 71st Cong., 3d Sess., February 28, 1931.

[19] H. Res. 404, 73d Cong., 2d Sess., June 15, 1934.

[20] S. Res. 114, 74th Cong., 1st Sess., August 24, 1935.

[21] S. Res. 246, 71st Cong., 2d Sess., April 17, 1930; and H. Res. 237, 73d Cong., 2d Sess., January 29, 1934.

[22] H. Res. 235, 72d Cong., 1st Sess., May 31, 1932.

[23] S. Res. 36, 75th Cong., 1st Sess., June 10, 1937.

(a) Research Investigations. With respect to the research inquiries, a varied choice of possible investigating mechanisms is presented. For example, the use of permanent staffs of advisory "experts" attached to Congressional standing committees may be a partial solution to the problem of obtaining information. The legislators thus could be relieved of much of the staggering detail. But the desirable insulation between the committee and the investigators would not be effected. The experts' conclusions would perhaps be guided by their employers' opinions.

One of the recent significant developments in the United States relating to legislative fact-finding is the growth of the legislative council. Since the creation of the first council in Wisconsin in 1931, students of government have become increasingly interested in the device.[24] In general, the principal duty of a legislative council—which is composed, at least in part, of representatives of both houses of the legislature[25]—is to select topics and to assemble material for the consideration of the legislature.[26] It is thus designed to enable the legislature to act intelligently, effectively, and without unnecessary delays. The council, working between sessions, makes a preliminary analysis of the factual material and presents its recommendations, perhaps in the form of drafts of bills, to the ensuing session of the legislative assembly. A research staff is generally attached to the council. The accomplishments of these agencies, it must

[24] Nine legislative councils have been established—in Wisconsin, Michigan, Kansas, Virginia, Kentucky, Nebraska, Connecticut, Illinois, and, on April 3, 1939, Maryland. See Martha J. Ziegler, "Legislators Work Between Sessions," 10 State Government 236 (1937) and Fred C. Kelly, "Government by Test-Tube," 49 Current History 35 (1939).

[25] All legislative councils are not cast from the same die. Some consist of the executive and legislators and perhaps laymen; others, as in Michigan and Kansas, include only legislators.

[26] The chief duty of the Wisconsin council, however, is to advise the governor on any subject he may refer to it; see Hubert R. Gallagher, "Legislative Councils," 24 National Municipal Review 147 (1935). The supervisory possibilities of legislative councils are also significant; see infra, p. 141, footnote.

be admitted, have, in a number of instances, been disappointing. Because the legislatures have shown some reluctance to accept the proposals which the legislative councils make, the councils have, on the whole, not yet attained the success predicted. The device does, however, show promise. Whether it should or could be transplanted from the state to the nation presents a separate question; [27] suffice it to say that it should be borne in mind, in any consideration of the advisability of such action, that the principal function of a legislative council may be performed by a strong Executive who takes the lead in formulating the legislative policy. Whether Congress should or should not adopt the scheme, however, is not the question of primary importance in a discussion of inquiries. The cardinal point concerns rather the process of investigation. If the device were put into practice nationally, the same investigatory principles should apply with respect to a legislative council as to Congress itself or to a committee of Congress—the inquiring agencies should in many instances be detached from the council, and the council should, rather than assume an inquiring role, pass judgment on the conclusions submitted by others. Thus, the action of the Michigan legislative council in handling the problem of the control of liquor in 1933 serves as an example of commendable procedure. A " subcommittee ", containing no members of the council, was asked to recommend legislation; following its investigation, which included public hearings, it drafted a bill for submission to the council which in turn considered the proposals in executive session and made revisions.[28]

Among the other possibilities for research agencies is an advisory or " national economic " council. The economic councils in existence throughout the world vary widely as to their duties and their method of composition. Thus, Lewis L. Lorwin

---

[27] Two features of most of the state legislatures may make the need for a legislative council more pressing in a state than in the federal government: (1) the biennial sessions, and (2) the rapid turnover of the members.

[28] Harold M. Dorr, "A Legislative Council for Michigan," 28 *American Political Science Review* 270 (1934).

has grouped them into three main types:[29] the "regulatory planning type;"[30] the "representative advisory type" which are "composed of representatives of the different economic groups of the country and whose function is primarily that of advising the legislature and the government on economic and social matters;" and the "appointed consultative type" which include "committees and councils . . . composed either entirely of government officials, or partly of private persons and partly of government officials, and which are attached to the government . . . for purposes of consultation and technical information." Much can be said for the desirability in the federal government of a permanent agency, with a broad overall view, which would be empowered to draw up plans and recommendations for the consideration of the legislature, and which could be consulted by Congress on particular problems. Such a group, providing a continuity of research, could perhaps help to overcome the defects of spotty and haphazard study. It should be equipped with a highly technical staff and have the means to obtain the help of the best available intelligence. Whether the council were, in Mr. Lorwin's language, a representative advisory type or an appointed consultative type, it might prove to be, if it remained impartial and did not try to control policy, a useful instrument by which the knowledge of experts could be applied to the problems confronting Congress. Although the advisory council has to date remained foreign to the United States, it has received consideration in Congress. A subcommittee of the Senate's Committee on Manufactures, for instance, conducted a study from 1935 to 1939 of the "advisability of establishing an economic council."[31] It would be risky, nevertheless, to predict that an

[29] Lewis L. Lorwin, *Advisory Economic Councils* (Washington, The Brookings Institution, 1931), p. 8. Also see A. N. Holcombe, *Government in a Planned Democracy* (New York, W. W. Norton & Co., 1935), p. 151.

[30] The "regulatory" type of council is not considered in this study.

[31] S. Res. 114, 74th Cong., 1st Sess., August 24, 1935. A suggested outline of the general form which a "National Economic Council" should take was presented in a Confidential Senate Committee Print of the 75th Cong., 3d

advisory council will be created. Indeed, the problems connected with the establishment of such a council—questions of size, of appointment, of term of office, of dismissal, of coordination with the executive agencies, of whether the council would originate studies or would confine itself to subjects presented to it by the President or Congress—are so difficult that cautiousness would seem to be advisable. The present National Resources Planning Board, however,—although its field is restricted [32]—may be characterized as a sort of economic council. It is composed of administrators and of persons not regularly in the government service and it has been aided by a permanent as well as by special temporary staffs.

Sess. (1938), "Statement of Senator Robert J. Bulkley, Chairman of the Committee on Manufactures, Concerning a National Economic Council or National Council," printed for the use of the Committee on Manufactures. The committee was instructed (S. Res. 281, 75th Cong., 3d Sess., June 16, 1938) to submit its final report by June 30, 1939. Senator Bulkley, who introduced the original resolution of authorization, was, however, not returned to the Senate in the elections of November 1938. Senator Overton, his successor as chairman, wrote on April 18, 1939, in answer to an inquiry from the writer as to the committee's progress with the study: "the Senate Committee on Manufactures resolved on March 2, 1939, indefinitely to postpone consideration and preparation of a bill to establish a National Economic Council. All of the documents in connection therewith, were, at the request of former Senator Bulkley . . . delivered to him in order that he might employ them as he deemed proper."

See also *Establishment of National Economic Council*, Hearings on Senate Bill No. 6215, 71st Cong., October 22 to December 19, 1931, Committee on Manufactures.

[32] It is empowered to make studies concerning the land, water, mineral, and "other national resources," and such related subjects as the President may refer to it. The board was first set up by Administrator Ickes as a National Planning Board attached to the Public Works Administration. Later it was established by Executive Order No. 6777, June 30, 1934, as the National Resources Board. No essential changes were made when it became the National Resources Committee under Executive Order No. 7065, June 7, 1935. It was consolidated with the Federal Employment Stabilization Office, transferred to the Executive Office of the President, and renamed the National Resources Planning Board, on July 1, 1939, by authority of President Roosevelt's "reorganization plan No. I" (H. Doc. 262, 76th Cong., 1st Sess.) of April 25, 1939 and S. J. Res. 138, 76th Cong., 1st Sess.

The National Resources Planning Board (or its predecessors) has conducted a number of significant studies, both on its own initiative and at the request of the President. In 1935, for example, the National Resources Committee issued, in accordance with a Presidential request, a report dealing with " important problems of planning and development which overlap State lines or which require the use of combined Federal and State powers." [33] For this study, a special research staff of six members was set up under the general direction of a technical committee on regional planning which was composed of two professors of political science, the planning consultant to the states of Wisconsin and Michigan, and a member of the permanent staff of the National Resources Committee. A report on " Public Works Planning " [34] was also issued at the instance of the President. Prepared by two divisions of the National Resources Committee—the water resources committee and the division of costs research—the report recommended a policy for " planning, programming, timing, and division of costs of public works." The Committee offered a list of public works projects which were intended to provide " a reservoir of undertakings " to cover a period of at least ten years. A third example of the significant reports prepared under the auspices of the National Resources Committee was a study of " The Problems of a Changing Population." [35] In this instance the Committee's science committee—which was composed of " designees from the National Academy of Sciences, the Social Science Research Council, and the American Council of Education "—set up a special subcommittee of six to supervise the research. This supervisory subcommittee consisted of three professors from the science committee, two other members who were in no way connected with the government, and the economist in charge of the division of land economics of the United States Bureau of Agricultural Economics. The report discussed

[33] *Regional Factors in National Planning and Development* (1935).
[34] *Public Works Planning* (1936).
[35] *The Problems of a Changing Population* (1938).

a number of the "problems which must be faced within the next generation;" some of the subjects treated were the trends in population, the changing age groups, migration, health, education, and the economic opportunity. The high calibre of these and other studies by the National Resources Committee will hardly be questioned. Much of the information was, of course, of value to Congress. It would seem to be desirable that Congress should have a permanent agency to which it could entrust some of the research inquiries that are now conducted by the Congressional committees. Since the National Resources Planning Board has already built considerable prestige for itself, Congress's first steps in the direction of meeting this need might well be to make the Board permanent and to expand its field. Gradually, then, the Board might be developed into a vast informational clearing house for the use of both Congress and the President.[36]

Still another alternative suggestion calls for investigations by *ad hoc* public or semi-public commissions. It would seem to be advisable that more research inquiries should be put in charge of groups which are patterned on the lines of the British Royal Commissions or departmental committees.[37] To urge this

[36] A bill which was introduced in the seventy-fourth Congress would have placed the National Resources Committee on a permanent basis and broadened its field. See the debate as well as the hearing on S. 2825. *National Planning Board Act of 1935*, Hearing before the Committee on Commerce, U. S. Senate, 74th Cong., 1st Sess., on S. 2825, June 13, 1935. The President's Committee on Administrative Management also recommended (*Report with Special Studies*, p. 29) that a committee be created to serve as a permanent "central planning agency under the President." Neither of these proposals contemplated Congressional requests to the committee for information. The Executive's real need for a general staff is not questioned; but Congress, it would seem, if it should establish a permanent "National Resources Planning Board," should retain for itself the privilege of asking that board to conduct an inquiry for some special purpose. While occasional conflicts might arise if both the Executive and Congress use the same group of experts, little serious discord should result.

[37] H. M. Clokie and J. W. Robinson, in the only recent book-length discussion of Royal Commissions, point to the similarities of the Royal Commissions and the departmental committees: "The only difference between

action is not to overlook the Commissions' imperfections. England's Commissions cannot be considered a final solution of all the investigatory problems. An exaggerated awe of the British device by some Americans must be tempered by an understanding of its deficiencies. The Commissions' blue books, for instance, are not uncommonly brown with age before the results, if any, are observable. Moreover, criticism has attended the alleged dominance of some inquiring groups by a " governing class " stratum with leanings toward a maintenance of the status quo.[38] Other Commissions are derided as governmental tools for the purpose of shelving a subject or of evading criticism. Sidney and Beatrice Webb have frowned upon the preponderance of oral " evidence " in some inquiries —unverified " evidence " which is obtained by members unskilled in the difficult art of interviewing, and which now and then comprises nothing more than opinions elicited for use in supporting the recommendations in the eventual report.[39]

The Royal Commission pattern is elastic. Some groups are composed chiefly of technical experts; others, established on the basis of bringing " fresh " minds to a problem, include members chosen from the ranks of the so-called impartial or indifferent; very occasionally, a group consists of members of Parliament. Generally in recent years, however, an effort is made to enlist representatives of each principal interest concerned. Although each method of choice, or a combination of the methods, may appear to be the most satisfactory for Congressional use in particular instances, the inclination of the British, after a long experience, to favor a representative selection should bear considerable weight.

the departmental committee and a Royal Commission, for all practical purposes, is that the former lacks the aura of dignity and eminence to be derived from the title of a 'Royal Commission' and the possession of a royal warrant of appointment." *Royal Commissions of Inquiry* (Stanford University, Stanford University Press, 1937), p. 207.

[38] H. F. Gosnell, "British Royal Commissions of Inquiry," 49 *Political Science Quarterly* 84 (1934).

[39] *Methods of Social Study* (London, Longmans, 1932), chap. VII.

The Royal Commissions, in spite of some defects, provide an impressive record. Felix Frankfurter has asserted that " the history of British democracy might in considerable measure be written in terms of the history of successive Royal Commissions." [40] Their prestige is unquestionable. Citizens of the highest type have gladly served as members. Indeed, the tradition of Royal Commissions is so important as to cast a shadow of doubt on the possibilities of successfully transplanting the device to foreign soil. But scattered experiences indicate that the Royal Commission seedling can thrive elsewhere.

The National Monetary Commission created in 1908,[41] for example, may be called to mind. Established as a direct consequence of the panic of 1907 to recommend " necessary or desirable (changes) in the monetary system or in the laws relating to banking and currency," it submitted a final report only after three and a half years of broad study. The detachment of the investigators in this case was not absolute—the Commission itself was composed of eighteen legislators with Senator Aldrich as chairman and Representative Vreeland as vice-chairman. But the Congressmen depended on others for the accumulation of most of the information. Professors, bankers, and experts in the monetary problems of the United States and foreign countries were commissioned to prepare analyses of specialized aspects of the subject. Altogether, the Commission issued twenty-three volumes of publications, three-fourths of which might be called treatises by experts.[42] Hearings, significantly, were seldom conducted. Some members of the Commission visited Canada and six European nations to glean less than two volumes of orderly questions and answers which were termed " interviews "; the personalities of these investigators, contrary to custom, were submerged, since the records failed to specify the names of the individual interrogators. The only recorded hearings in the United States were confined to two

---

[40] *The Public and Its Government* (New Haven, Yale University Press, 1930), p. 162.

[41] 35 Stat. 552.

[42] See *supra*, p. 13.

days. The legislative results of the Monetary Commission's work speak well for the care and prudence in the procedure; the final report was an important influence on the federal reserve act.

The Advisory Council on Social Security is a more recent example of an extra-governmental investigating committee. The manner of its creation was unusual. The Senate's Committee on Finance agreed on February 22, 1937 that the chairman of the committee should appoint a special subcommittee to cooperate with the Social Security Board in studying the advisability of amending the social security act. It was also agreed that this special committee, together with the Social Security Board, would select an Advisory Council on Social Security to " assist " in the study. The Advisory Council, appointed in May 1937, consisted of twenty-five members, six representing labor, six representing employers, and thirteen representing the public. The Council in turn chose an " interim committee," composed of two members each from the labor and employer representatives, and three from the public group, to make a continuous study of the problems before the Council and to draw up the agenda for the plenary sessions of the Council. The Social Security Board furnished the necessary technical assistance to the interim committee. The Advisory Council, holding meetings at intervals of a few months, issued its report in December 1938 in time for the consideration of the seventy-sixth Congress.[43]

The executive has in recent years made a wider use of public or semi-public commissions of inquiry than has Congress. President Hoover frequently created *ad hoc* groups for study. Two of the more noted examples of his commissions were the President's Research Committee on Social Trends and the National Commission on Law Observance and Enforcement (Wickersham Commission). Mr. Hoover was by no means a pioneer in the field, but the extent of his utilization of *ad hoc*

[43] S. Doc. 4, 76th Cong., 1st Sess. (report dated December 10, 1938). The report was signed by all the members of the Council, although a few reservations were attached.

commissions was probably unprecedented. During his first three years in the White House he created thirty-eight commissions, of which seven received some appropriation for their work, while the others were voluntary or were supported by public institutions.[44] While some of these commissions were lauded as scientific approaches to the solution of public problems, the excessive use tended to discredit the method. The critics maintained, moreover, that the procedure frequently formed a device for shelving a subject pending the diversion of the public's interest.[45]

[44] W. S. Myers and W. H. Newton, *The Hoover Administration* (New York, C. Scribner's Sons, 1936), p. 492. Although the members of a temporary public commission may serve without pay, other expenses may of course be incurred in connection with an inquiry. The financing of an *ad hoc* commission is, therefore, generally an important problem to be met. For the government to make a practice of conducting inquiries with private funds does not, for obvious reasons, seem to be sound.

Because Congress holds the purse strings, the President's problem of where to find the money for an investigation may be especially troublesome. A President therefore may, in most cases, attempt to utilize government officials and employees to act as members of, or to provide assistance to, the *ad hoc* investigating bodies which he appoints. President Roosevelt has, on several occasions, created commissions composed partly of government men and partly of persons not regularly in the government service. The funds for such a semi-public commission may come from a source which is applicable only to the particular inquiry in question. For example, the President's Committee of Industrial Analysis (consisting of the Secretaries of Commerce, Agriculture, and Labor and four members from outside the government), which was created in 1936 to prepare a review of the results of the National Recovery Administration, was authorized to supervise the expenditure of $100,000 that was transferred by the President from the funds available to the Department of Commerce under the emergency relief appropriation act of 1935.

[45] Senator Norris turned poet to express his disapprobation:

> Once to every man and nation
> Comes the moment to decide,
> In the strife of truth with falsehood,
> For the good or evil side.
> But the case presents no problem
> To the White House engineer;
> He appoints a big commission
> To report some time next year.

Quoted by Silas Bent in "Mr. Hoover's Sins of Commissions," 90 *Scribner's Magazine* 9 (1931).

In the light of this rather general attitude, President Roosevelt was reluctant to follow in his predecessor's footsteps. Under the new Administration, public and semi-public fact finding commissions were created with less frequency.[46] Several examples may be cited, however, of creditable inquiries that helped to increase the prestige of these *ad hoc* investigating commissions. Thus, the Committee on Economic Security was appointed by executive order on June 29, 1934.[47] Earlier in the month a Presidential message to Congress, which listed several goals in the " task of reconstruction," stated that " among our objectives I place the security of the men, women and children of the nation first." The Committee on Economic Security was asked to make recommendations on one aspect of security—safeguards " against misfortunes which cannot be wholly eliminated in this man-made world of ours." The arrangement of the personnel was novel. The committee proper consisted of four cabinet members and the Federal Emergency Relief Administrator. This committee obtained assistance by appointing, in accordance with the executive order, a technical board on economic security which was composed of twenty-one persons in the government service who had a special interest in or knowledge of various aspects of the problem. The President also selected an " advisory council " of twenty-three private citizens representing employers, employees, and the general public to aid in weighing the proposals developed by the staff.[48] In addition, the central committee employed a small staff of experts to prepare studies, and created seven other advisory groups to assist in the individual fields. The report, submitted on January 15, 1935, together with valuable appendant statis-

[46] President Roosevelt, as has been seen, has requested studies by the National Resources Committee of a number of broad problems.

[47] Executive Order No. 6757. For a detailed account of the " origins, operations, and effectiveness " of this committee, see Mary F. Trackett Reynolds, *Interdepartmental Committees in the National Administration* (New York, Columbia University Press, 1939).

[48] The advisory council assembled in Washington on four occasions for meetings which extended several days.

tics on the security laws of foreign countries and on the breadth of the problem in the United States,[49] became a guide for the social security act [50] which was approved later in the same year.

The Great Plains Committee, while it was essentially a commission of government officials, may, since it included in its membership a representative from the National Resources Committee, be considered with the semi-public commissions. President Roosevelt, in a letter of September 17, 1936, appointed a committee of eight to prepare a " land use program " for better protection against drought in the great plains. Morris L. Cooke, the administrator of the Rural Electrification Administration, was selected as the chairman; the other seven members were drawn from the water resources committee of the National Resources Committee, the Soil Conservation Service, the Resettlement Administration, the Works Progress Administration, the Corps of Engineers of the Army, the Bureau of Reclamation, and the Rural Electrification Administration. The committee, after holding hearings in two states as well as in the District of Columbia, and after pursuing studies in cooperation with several federal agencies and with state and regional planning bodies, submitted a report [51] in February 1937 which recommended specific organized action by the federal, state, and county governments and by the individual farmers.[52]

49 Committee on Economic Security, *Report to the President* (1935).

50 49 Stat. 620.

51 H. Doc. 144, 75th Cong., 1st Sess., February 10, 1937, *The Future of the Great Plains.*

52 Two days after he had requested the study by the Great Plains Committee, the President wrote to Secretary of Agriculture Wallace proposing a study of crop insurance. The Committee on Crop Insurance, as appointed by the President, consisted only of government officials. Mr. Wallace was designated as the chairman. The President specifically requested that the committee's " final recommendations for legislation should be formulated with the advice and assistance of national farm organization leaders so that the plans can be submitted to Congress, with the approval and support of the representatives of the farmers." The report (President's Committee on Crop Insurance, *Report and Recommendations*, December 1936) formed

A comprehensive analysis of " the entire field of educational service in the United States " was begun in 1936 by a semi-public commission of twenty-three members which was established by the President. The study was an outgrowth of a bill [53] passed by the seventy-fourth Congress which authorized an increase, beginning July 1, 1937, in the federal contributions to the states for vocational education. The President directed the committee to " study the experience under the existing program of Federal aid for vocational education, the relation of such training to general education and to prevailing economic and social conditions, and the extent of the need for an expanded program . . . to develop recommendations which will be available to the Congress and to the Executive." A supplementary letter by the President on April 19, 1937 asked the committee " to give more extended consideration to the whole subject of Federal relationship to State and local conduct of education." A professor of education from the University of Chicago, Floyd W. Reeves, was selected as the chairman. The committee was composed of representatives of four governmental departments and the Tennessee Valley Authority, as well as private authorities in a variety of fields which included education, industry, labor, and agriculture. This group organized a temporary staff of specialists in education, public administration, and economics, and enlisted the cooperation of numerous educators and of agencies both in the government and in the educational field. The members of the committee attended meetings and conferences that " aggregated more than forty days." The final report [54] pointed to the great need for improvement in many of the public schools and in the rural areas generally. Recommendations were made that the federal government increase its financial aid for schooling. The report con-

the general basis for the crop insurance provisions of the agricultural act of 1938 (52 Stat. 31).

[53] 49 Stat. 1488, June 8, 1936.

[54] The Advisory Committee on Education, *Report of the Committee* (February 1938). Nineteen " staff studies " were also published.

templated an ultimate consolidation of federal aid for vocational education with general federal aid for elementary and secondary education.

Perhaps one of the most significant of the recent studies by an *ad hoc* commission was that by the President's Special Committee on Farm Tenancy. President Roosevelt, in a letter of November 16, 1936, asked the Secretary of Agriculture to serve as the chairman of a committee to prepare a report suggesting " a long term program of action to alleviate the shortcomings of our farm tenancy system." It was the President's thought " that the first step in evolving a workable program is the preparation, under the general auspices of the National Resources Committee, of a comprehensive report by a special committee of persons who have both an extensive knowledge of the problem and a sympathetic interest in its solution." An elaborate investigatory device was set up. The President chose a committee of forty-one members, of which eight were government officials. He also designated Dr. L. C. Gray, the assistant administrator of the Resettlement Administration, to serve as the executive secretary and technical director of the committee. The " special " committee, together with the National Resources Committee, then selected a " technical committee " of eight members to make a study and to draft a report. Five of the members of the technical committee, in addition to Dr. Gray who was made its chairman, were drawn from the President's committee. The technical committee was, therefore, a representative body which was composed of three government officials and five representatives of the public. This subcommittee obtained information and help from a variety of sources. Dr. Mordecai Ezekiel, economic adviser to the Secretary of Agriculture, attended its meetings and assisted it in its work. Hearings were held at five central points where the tenancy problem was serious. The members also held consultations with the advisory committee of the National Resources Committee. Moreover, much of the technical material which was used by the committee was, according to the report, assembled by the land use planning section of the Resettlement Administration, with the assistance of specialists from the Bureau of Agricultural Economics, the Social Security Board, and other agencies. The final report [55] as issued to the President, although it was accompanied by the dissents of five members, was approved with a high degree of unanimity by the President's committee.[56] The President, on February 16, 1937, submitted the report to Congress. Some of the recommendations were included in the Bankhead-Jones farm tenancy bill which was approved five months later.[57]

President Roosevelt chose a committee of nine prominent citizens [58] in 1938 to investigate the employer-employee relationships in Great Britain. This group closely corresponded to a British Royal Commission. Although requests for a change in the existing labor laws had been voiced by employers and by a segment of labor, Mr. Roosevelt vigorously denied any intentions of a revision. Irrespective of the immediate purposes, however, a study befitted a subject which was widely misunderstood as a result of conflicting reports. The conditions in Sweden were included in the survey later. The members of the committee, selected on the basis of a representation of interests, with no designation of a chairman, were drawn from organized labor,[59] industry, and the public. Organized in June 1938, this Commission on Industrial Relations quietly pursued its studies abroad, where it held conferences with the officials

[55] President's Committee on Farm Tenancy, *Report of the President's Committee* (February 1937).

[56] The dissents, the most important of which was written by a representative of the Southern Tenant Farmers' Union, related merely to individual items in the report.

[57] 50 Stat. 522, July 22, 1937.

[58] The invitations to serve on the committee were issued by the Secretary of Labor, but the acceptances were acknowledged by the President.

[59] Although the American Federation of Labor was represented, President Lewis of the Committee for Industrial Organization, suspecting an attempt to modify the national labor relations act, refused to accept the Administration's invitation to designate an emissary.

of employers' associations, trade unions, and the government. Two reports, one on Great Britain and one on Sweden,[60] submitted in September, received wide praise for their thoroughness and impartiality—further evidence of the possible effectiveness of such *ad hoc* groups in the research field.

(b) Inquisitorial Investigations. The quality of a number of the recent studies by the public or semi-public temporary commissions and by the National Resources Committee would seem to support the proposal that Congress might well delegate some of its research inquiries to *ad hoc* commissions on the order of British Royal Commissions, and to a central advisory agency or economic council which might be built around the National Resources Planning Board. As has been suggested, however, these investigatory devices may not be adaptable to the inquiries which have been characterized as inquisitorial, where the investigating agency's power to compel the disclosure of information is especially important. It is offered for consideration, therefore, that Congress's burdens should perhaps be lightened by a more frequent delegation of the inquisitorial inquiries to administrative bodies. A Congressional resolution might direct a department or bureau, for example, to conduct an inquiry within its own particular field. Thus, the Treasury Department, as the President suggested, might have handled the investigation of the avoidance of income taxes.[61] The Department of Justice, moreover, should perhaps carry more of the probing load in such a situation as this. Although the inquiring committees of Congress not uncommonly refer the material which they unearth to the Attorney General for his follow-up,[62] only rarely does the Senate or the House, by a resolution, request the initiation of an investigation by the Department.[63] As a

[60] Commission on Industrial Relations in Great Britain, *Report* (1938), and Commission on Industrial Relations in Sweden, *Report* (1938).

[61] See *supra*, p. 26.

[62] See *supra*, p. 89.

[63] An example of a request for an investigation by the Department of Justice was S. Res. 220, 71st Cong., 2d Sess., introduced by Senator Wheeler:

general rule, however, the regulatory commissions, because they are vested with the control of many of the nation's major economic matters, would appear to be the preferable agencies for conducting some of the inquisitorial investigations for Congress.[64] The commissions have the advantage, not enjoyed by all the executive agencies, of having staffs already assembled for investigatorial purposes. Moreover, two of the commissions' features—the board structure and the " independence " —although they are sometimes criticized as not promoting effective administration, should help to gain the public's confidence in the investigations which the commissions conduct. Thus, agencies like the Federal Trade Commission, the Interstate Commerce Commission, the Securities and Exchange Commission, the Federal Communications Commission, the Federal Power Commission, and the National Labor Relations Board appear to be suited for undertaking inquiries, at the request of Congress, in their individual areas of interest.

It must be admitted at the outset that the advisability of putting an inquisitorial inquiry in charge of a regulatory agency may be questioned sometimes because of the possibility that the investigation may interfere with the agency's administrative work. Thus, an inquiry by a commission may tend to destroy the prestige and the good will which that commission has worked hard to build. Much of the federal regulation of business is successfully accomplished in a spirit of friendly cooperation between the government and business. The Federal Trade Commission's trade practice conferences offer a case in

" Resolved, That the Attorney General of the United States be, and he is hereby, requested to make an investigation of the corporations and associations engaged in the business of selling oil and gasoline in the State of Montana, for the purpose of determining whether any such corporations or associations are fixing prices or engaged in other practices in violation of the Federal anti-trust laws."

[64] This and the succeeding statements are made on the assumption that the independent regulatory commissions will continue to function on substantially the same basis, and to occupy virtually the same position in the governmental structure, as at present. It is recognized, however, that the future of the commissions is not settled.

point. The extent to which it is desirable to cultivate this friend-
liness is a problem; it obviously may be carried to extremes.
Nevertheless, if a regulatory body is asked to conduct an investigation of those persons with whom it commonly deals, a
marked hostility between the two conceivably may be fostered.
Congress, before asking for such an investigation, should consider this possible consequence and judge its importance. It
would seem, however, that, despite this objection to the delegation of some of the inquisitorial investigations to the regulatory commissions, a number of inquiries could be turned over
to them without impairing the performance of the commissions'
regular duties. Indeed, a commission might find its good will
enhanced if its investigation should lead to the eradication of
wrong-doing which had been practiced by only a small per-
centage of those persons under inquiry.[65]

GENERAL DELEGATION OF SUPERVISORY INQUIRIES NOT DE-
SIRABLE. By the delegation of many of the research and inquisitorial inquiries Congress may conserve its investigatorial
strength principally for the scrutinies in pursuance of its supervisory function. No convincing argument is presented for a
general delegation in this field. In order to discharge effectively
its " board of directors ' " duties, Congress, it would seem,
should retain for its own committees the conduct of the investigations of the executive. Thus, it may have a better opportunity
to parallel the benefits of the close contact between the legislature and the executive which is maintained by the question
time in England, and by interpellation and the parliamentary

[65] Those persons who object to the delegation of inquiries to the independent regulatory commissions may also argue that the members of the
commissions are so overworked that they can handle additional investigations no better than can Congress. There are, it is true, heavy burdens on
these commissions. The National Labor Relations Board, for example, has
to date been so entangled in the administration of the Wagner labor act as
to raise the question of the wisdom of burdening it further by Congressional
requests for inquiries. Speaking generally, however, these groups would
appear to be capable of complying with a reasonable number of such demands.

commissions in France.[66] An effectual supervision, however, may require investigations supplementary to those by Congressional committees. Two devices merit consideration. The first is an auditing agency. The budget and accounting act of 1921 represented an attempt to meet this demand by the creation of an independent Comptroller General's office. Since one of the functions of the Comptroller General was to be the making of inquiries for Congress into the violations of the law in financial matters, a lessening of the need for investigations of the executive branch by Congressional committees was anticipated. But the failure of the act to distinguish between control from within the administration and audit from without, led to a dissipation of the agency's functions.[67] The efforts of the Comptroller General were concentrated on passing advance judgments on the validity of payments. His submission of reports to Congress on the " financial accountability of the administrative heads," consequently, was " almost completely overlooked." [68] The apparent breakdown of this phase of the budget and accounting act does not, however, justify pessimism over the efficacy of a genuine audit as a means of legislative control of the executive. An agency which was concerned only with postaudit would probably become a valuable investigatory tool for Congress.

A second reservation to the general principle of the inexpediency of delegating the supervisory inquiries may be occasioned by the possible advisability of strengthening the authority and responsibility of the executive head for unearthing

[66] See Lindsay Rogers, " Parliamentary Commissions in France," 38 *Political Science Quarterly* 413 and 602 (1923). The Congressional standing committees, of course, maintain supervision to some extent, but not to the degree possible if they were more articulated with the executive departments. A legislative council might exercise the same sort of intersessional supervision as a parliamentary commission does.

[67] See *supra*, p. 12.

[68] A. E. Buck, in President's Committee on Administrative Management, *Report with Special Studies* (1937), p. 159; also see Harvey C. Mansfield, *The Comptroller General* (New Haven, Yale University Press, 1939), chap. X.

the irregularities or incompetency in his administrative machine. Thus, the New York state legislature recognized the desirability of such action by its enactment in 1907 of the Moreland act. This law grants full power to the governor to investigate, " either in person or by one or more persons appointed by him, . . . the management and affairs " of any state executive agency.[69] The scheme has, on the whole, worked well in New York; the investigations which have been conducted under the act have effected a number of repairs necessitated by administrative breakdowns. A danger would appear to lie in the possible utilization of the law for whitewashing. The developments have, however, provided little ground for such skepticism; on the contrary, some of the inquiries have tended to dispel unfounded charges.

A federal " Moreland " act might prove to be similarly salutary. The Department of Justice may sometimes act in much the same capacity as a " Moreland " commissioner might, but it is always doubtful whether an investigation of an executive department or agency by another department will satisfy either Congress or the public. Thus, Secretary of the Interior Wilbur asked the Department of Justice in 1930 to investigate the " reckless and false statements " made by Ralph S. Kelley, a subordinate official within the Department of the Interior. Mr. Kelley, the chief of the field division of the General Land Office at Denver, resigned from his post on September 28, 1930 after

[69] *Laws of the State of New York*, 1907, Ch. 539, as amended by L. 1928, Ch. 131: " The governor is authorized at any time, either in person or by one or more persons appointed by him for the purpose, to examine and investigate the management and affairs of any department, board, bureau or commission of the state. The governor and persons so appointed by him are empowered to subpoena and enforce the attendance of witnesses, to administer oaths and examine witnesses under oath and to require the production of any books or papers deemed relevant or material. Whenever any person so appointed shall not be regularly in the service of the state his compensation for such services shall be fixed by the governor, and said compensation and all necessary expenses of such examinations and investigations shall be paid from the treasury out of any appropriations made for the purpose upon the order of the governor and the audit and warrant of the comptroller."

more than twenty-five years of service in the Department. At
the same time he charged that the Department, both before and
after the then current Administration took office, had submitted
to pressures brought by the oil interests and had allowed those
interests to obtain titles to the oil shale reserves on the public
domain in Colorado " by fraud and failure to comply with the
requirements of the United States mining laws." [70] Kelley declined to furnish to the Department of Justice's investigator,
Assistant Attorney General Richardson, the details of his alle-
gations,[71] but published his charges in a series of articles which
were syndicated by the *New York World*. The Department of
Justice, after its inquiry, reported on October 26 that there was
" no merit or substance " in the charges.[72] Mr. Kelley, however,
called the report a " ridiculous whitewash." By this time the
controversy had become so troublesome to the Administration
that President Hoover, at a press conference, saw fit to rebuke
Kelley. Senator Thomas J. Walsh, however, was one of the
Congressmen who were not fully convinced that an adequate
investigation of the matter had been made. On December 19,
therefore, he introduced a resolution [73] directing an investigation into the charges. Although the resolution was never
reported by the Committee on Public Lands and Surveys to
which it was referred, the consideration of the resolution by
the committee was in itself an investigation.[74] Indeed, Senator
Walsh, when he introduced the resolution, had explained: " I
shall ask that the resolution be referred to the Committee on
Public Lands and Surveys, which can, at little or no expense,
prosecute the necessary preliminary inquiry and make recommendations to the Senate as to the course that ought to be

[70] *New York Times*, September 29, 1930.

[71] Kelley insisted that Richardson had "prejudged the case."

[72] On the basis of this report, Secretary Wilbur accepted Kelley's resignation on October 29.

[73] S. Res. 379, 71st Cong., 3d Sess., December 19, 1930.

[74] *Oil Shale Lands*, Hearings before the Committee on Public Lands and
Surveys, U. S. Senate, 71st Cong., 3d Sess., on S. Res. 379, January 31,
February 3, 6, 10, 12, 26, and 27, 1931.

pursued with reference to the same." [75] Both Secretary Wilbur and Mr. Kelley were among the witnesses at this "preliminary" inquiry. No further action was taken following the hearings.[76]

Congress, therefore, may be assisted in its supervisory duties by inquiries which are pursued by an auditing agency or by the executive branch itself. It appears to be desirable, nevertheless, that, in general, the principal reliance for inquiries relating to supervision should be placed on Congressional committees which thereby can be the means of maintaining a close contact between the legislature and the administrators.

THE INVESTIGATORY PROCESS MUST REMAIN FLEXIBLE. Althought an attempt has been made to erect inquisitorial and research classifications as guides for determining the most desirable type of agency for conducting each investigation, it is evident that the compartments must not be sealed watertight. The inquiries cannot be pigeon-holed with a machine's precision. An investigation of un-American activities, for instance, may be catalogued as inquisitorial, and yet seem to befit study by an *ad hoc* commission rather than by any administrative body. Other inquisitorial probes may occasionally cover a field which is seemingly too vast for an executive agency; such was the inquiry into railroad financing which was piloted by a Senate committee partially because of doubts as to the authority of the Interstate Commerce Commission to investigate bankers.[77] Nor should the classifications remain so rigid as to pre-

[75] *Congressional Record*, 71st Cong., 3d Sess., p. 1081, December 19, 1930.

[76] Even before the hearings began, Senator Nye, the chairman of the Committee on Public Lands and Surveys, after a conference with Mr. Kelley, announced that Kelley was "quite justified" in making his charges. "I can't help but be impressed," he said, "by the spirit moving Mr. Kelley at this stage . . . (His) resignation and the fact that he will give the public the information he has, means that he is doing the only thing a public servant could do." The Senator asserted, however, that the charges did not "go to the door" of Secretary Wilbur, but rather went back to former Administrations. *New York Times*, October 4, 1930.

[77] See *infra*, p. 153.

vent the conduct of some research investigations by administrative bodies; there was no convincing objection, for instance, to the study of traffic conditions by a Department of Agriculture which included the Bureau of Public Roads.[78] Furthermore, the inquiries into subjects which are closely related to the behavior of the legislators themselves, while they are not always conducted in the most impartial or exhaustive manner, probably would gain little, if any, from being directed by outside agencies; [79] examples of such subjects are lobbying and campaign expenditures. Another type of exception is especially important and at the same time exceedingly difficult to isolate; the LaFollette committee's investigation of the infringements of civil liberties [80] will illustrate the point. The information which was sought here was deeply imbedded. No ordinary prying could work it loose. It seemed essential that the probers should have the benefits of prestige as well as a full investigatiory power. Senator LaFollette and his investigators were forced to tread on new ground, and, from the outset, had to prepare themselves for terrific onslaughts on their work. The findings were so startling in some instances as to foster popular incredulity rather than shock. Strike breaking and labor spying, for example, had been generally known to exist, but not to the extent here revealed.[81] Whether the committee went to excesses, and whether every scrap of information that they collected was authentic, are questions which, for the purposes of the immediate discussion, are beside the point. The conclusion to be drawn here is: the disclosures related to such delicate subjects, and were potentially so explosive, that

[78] 49 Stat. 1892, June 23, 1936.

[79] There is something to be said, however, for the British method of deciding the contested Parliamentary elections by a judicial inquiry. Although the House of Commons may overrule the opinion of the court, it customarily votes to approve. See Dimock, *op. cit.*, p. 70.

[80] S. Res. 266, 74th Cong., 2d Sess., June 6, 1936.

[81] The Commission on Industrial Relations of 1912 (see *supra*, p. 11), for instance, had called attention to these practices.

there is good reason to believe that other types of investigatory agencies either could not or would not have produced them.[82]

That the best agency for conducting a particular investigation cannot always be selected by a precise formula is also suggested by the Temporary National Economic Committee's so-called monopoly inquiry which began in 1938.[83] A sounder judgment on this investigation can be passed when the study is completed and a report is prepared; but, in the meantime, a few observations may be ventured. It should be remembered that the subject of the inquiry is extremely broad. It is scarcely debatable that no one administrative agency could satisfactorily handle it. A carefully selected public or semi-public commission might perhaps have been a wiser choice. In this instance, however, a genuine basis existed for President Roosevelt's suggestion of an inquiry to be conducted by the Federal Trade Commission, the Department of Justice, the Securities and Exchange Commission, and " such other agencies of the government as have special experience in various phases of the inquiry " : over a period of years an immense wealth of material which was pertinent to the subject had been amassed in individual bureaus and agencies, but no general analysis of this information had been made for the purpose of determining broad national policies. In other words, much of the material which was required for the investigation was already available, although it needed some means of coordination to enrich its value. Random examples of such information are the statistics on wages and on industrial prices, which are in the Department of Labor; the records of individual corporations with respect to the antitrust laws, which are in the Federal Trade Commission and the Department of Justice; the income tax reports of corporations and individuals and the information on identical bidding, which are in the Treasury Department; the varied

[82] See S. Rept. 46, 75th Cong., parts 1 to 4; S. Rept. 6, 76th Cong., 1st Sess., parts 1 to 4. The first of this series of reports was submitted on February 8, 1937.

[83] See *supra*, p. 41.

census figures, which are in the Department of Commerce; and the data on corporate ownership and control, which are in the Securities and Exchange Commission. But Congress, unwilling, as has been seen, to forego participation in the inquiry, approved a resolution which provided for the six and six division of membership on the committee.

Although dire predictions were made by some Congressmen and by a portion of the public as to the quality of the investigation which could be expected from this hybrid structure, it seems fair to say that the initial steps by the committee did not support the fears of the skeptics. Senator O'Mahoney appeared to be both capable and sincere in his role of chairman. An able coordinator also was chosen, who in turn assembled, exclusive of the clerks and secretaries, a staff of about one hundred experts. Without excessive fanfare, the involved task of collecting and dovetailing the information was begun, while the members of the committee and its staff offered reassurances to business. Comprehensive questionnaires, aimed at filling the gaps in the available data, were delivered to, among other groups, the trade associations and the life insurance companies. The early public hearings also inspired confidence in the inquiry. Purposely delayed until after the November 1938 elections, they were fully utilized for their bona fide purposes of providing an orderly, not a runaway, forum; and of clarifying, verifying, completing gaps in and spotlighting the information which was already collected.

Can the structure of the Temporary National Economic Committee be accepted, however, as a model for future investigations? Its extended use may not be practicable. While collaboration between the administrators and legislators is, in other respects, often desirable, its advantages in this instance are debatable. The chairman of the T. N. E. C., inferring that the committee was soundly built for investigating, emphasized that it was composed of members from " Congress which must eventually pass upon any legislation that may be recommended " and from the " executive agencies that are in closest relationship to the functioning of the economic machine." But a more judicious procedure would seem rather to require that those who " must eventually pass upon any legislation " should have the facts presented to them. Thus, basing their action on the reports prepared by others—in this instance, perhaps, by the six representatives of the agencies and departments, assisted by experts—they might avoid their own conscious or unconscious coloration of the data. Moreover, although the T. N. E. C. happily obtained an effective leader, a setup under which the chairman of an investigating group has no control over four-fifths of the purse appears to be, on the whole, a defect. This situation, coupled with a division of members between legis-lators and administrators, is an incentive to confusion and cross purposes. It may be argued that these provisions are a means for avoiding a rigged investigation; but the possible benefits of the provisions would seem to be overbalanced by the dis-order which they appear to invite. While the chairman of the T. N. E. C. has apparently been successful in forestalling any serious consequences of the potential division of authority on the committee, and while no wide rifts have to date developed in the group, the same harmony could hardly be predicted for any future attempts to employ the same setup. A modification in the arrangement whereby the expenditures were controlled at one point might aid materially in solving the problems of a division in the leadership, but discontent or even sabotage might at the same time be engendered. It seems to be a reasonable conclusion, therefore, that while the Temporary National Eco-nomic Committee's accomplishments may be outstanding, the device cannot be recommended for an extensive application in the future.

The admission that this hybrid arrangement may even oc-casionally appear to be suitable for an investigation furnishes additional evidence that, for the purposes of ascertaining the most fitting agency for a particular inquiry, a rigid formula cannot be invoked; flexibility must prevail. If this is fully real-ized, however, the suggested classification of investigations into two groups, research and inquisitorial, should prove to be a workable guide.

DELEGATION ENCOUNTERS OBSTACLES. The proposal that Congress should more frequently entrust its investigations to other agencies is made with the full realization that only faltering steps along these lines can be expected in the near future. The Senators and Representatives, acting as their own umpires in the selection of the devices, tend to confine investigations to legislative committees.

In attempting to analyze the forces operating against Congress's delegation of its investigations, it should be borne in mind that the political pressure against such action is strong, due primarily to the reluctance of the legislators to sacrifice the possible wealth of publicity which the inquiries can bring to them.[84] Readily understandable as an entirely human reaction, this attitude is perhaps heightened by a prosecution complex on the part of some of the lawyers who predominate in both the Senate and House.[85] A Congressional fear or jealousy of the growing power of the Executive may likewise be contributory. That the democracies since the World War have, generally speaking, leaned toward an expansion of executive, often at the expense of legislative, authority, is incontestable. It can also be argued that the same process is to some extent occurring in the United States.[86] Individuals may disagree as to its reality or its advisability, but a segment of Congress is ever alert to counteract such a trend. Thus, the legislators may be disinclined to transfer to other agencies any portion of so imposing a power as investigation. Moreover, the success of some executive inquiries may only impel Congressional emulation.

Congress also may be inclined to retain its full investigatory role because of the alleged deficiencies of other bodies in con-

[84] See *supra*, p. 45.

[85] See *supra*, p. 82.

[86] Reference is made to the long time trend, not merely to a single Administration.

ducting investigations. The group of inquiries, illustrated by the probe into the infringements of civil liberties, which Congressmen can perhaps handle more effectively than any other agency,[87] is, however, doubtless magnified in the average legislator's mind. Thus, an unwillingness to delegate the authority to investigate may arise from a belief that a Congressional committee forms a better sounding board. The importance of the social leverage aspect of Congressional inquiries has already been emphasized.[88] A rather general legislative attitude as to the competency of outside investigators to perform this function is illustrated by a statement of Representative Boileau. The subject of discussion was a resolution authorizing an investigation of an alleged " superlobby," the American Retail Federation.[89] The opposition to the resolution came from a minority which insisted that the inquiry could accomplish only a replowing of the ground already covered by the Federal Trade Commission's investigation of chain stores.[90] But Mr. Boileau argued otherwise: " The Federal Trade Commission has performed a very valuable service. . . . I believe that their investigations are of immeasurable benefit to the people of the country. I commend them for their report on the chain store investigation. I think they have put into the record some very valuable information, but I say to the Membership of this House that if we ever expect to arouse public opinion in this country, if we ever expect to have the people of this country stand back of and support legislation in the interest of the independent merchants of our country, if we expect the people of this country to demand that the Congress of the United States enact legislation that will prohibit secret rebates and other advantages being given by the manufacturers to the chain stores, then we must do something in addition to what the

[87] See *supra*, p. 145.

[88] See *supra*, p. 30.

[89] H. Res. 203, 74th Cong., 1st Sess., April 24, 1935.

[90] S. Res. 224, 70th Cong., 1st Sess. The final of thirty-three separate reports was submitted on December 14, 1934.

Federal Trade Commission has done. We must bring this matter out into the open. . . . We must bring this out from under cover." [91] The contention that a Congressional committee is a better informant is, however, at least debatable. It is safe to say that the House committee in this particular instance commanded no greater attention than had the Federal Trade Commission. Moreover, there are significant examples of delegated inquiries which have been well publicized. Thus, in the investigation of the American Telephone and Telegraph Company by the Federal Communications Commission [92] the hearings and reports gained choice newspaper space and prompted wide discussions. The Federal Trade Commission's extended study of the electric and gas public utility corporations was also outstanding.[93] Senator Walsh's original proposal for this investigation had suggested that it be directed by a select committee of the Senate. The utilities vigorously fought any form of inquiry but, when an investigation became inevitable, they strongly urged that it be conducted by the Trade Commission rather than by a committee. Thus, they hoped for more quiet and ineffectual proceedings. They were victorious, but their supposed advantage was minimized by a shrewd modification, first introduced by Senator Black, which provided for public hearings: " any such inquiry before the Commission to be open to the public and due notice of time and place of all hearings to be given by the Commission, and the stenographic report of the evidence taken by the Commission to accompany the partial and final reports." The investigation, aided by an aggressively competent counsel, assumed a national significance; it gained considerably greater prominence, for example, than the inquiry which was begun six years later by the House Committee on Interstate and Foreign Commerce into the ownership and control of the public utility corporations by holding companies.[94]

[91] *Congressional Record*, 74th Cong., 1st Sess., p. 12658, August 7, 1935.

[92] 49 Stat. 43, March 15, 1935.

[93] S. Res. 83, 70th Cong., 1st Sess., February 13, 1928.

[94] H. Res. 59, 72d Cong., 1st Sess., January 19, 1932.

The sounding-board properties of the Senate may be greater than those of the House.   But the differences in the informing capacities of even the Senate's committees as opposed to outside agencies are, it would seem, not sufficient to render one group generally more desirable than the other for investigating.

A more concrete motivation of the Congressional hesitancy to entrust an investigation to another body may emanate from a want of confidence in its personnel. This attitude may not amount to a positive disesteem; it may originate from nothing more than a legislator's sincere belief in his own talent for conducting the investigation in question. But, on the other hand, it may spring from an outright distrust. Thus, some Senators and Representatives probably feared that, unless members of Congress were included on the Temporary National Economic Committee, the business interests might not be given a full opportunity to present their case and to have a fair hearing. It is at least debatable, however, whether there are grounds for believing that, as a general rule, a witness will receive more sympathetic treatment before a committee of Congressmen than before an administrative agency. Moreover, the likelihood that the witnesses will be given a chance to have their say before a non-Congressional inquiring group probably will be increased if Congress directs that the hearings shall not be private.

The distrust of the personnel of an investigating body may be of particular consequence with respect to the inquisitorial inquiries at a time when the social philosophies of the administrative agencies and of Congress may lie far apart. The independent commissions provide a case in point. It is hardly surprising, for instance, that in 1932 a House which was organized by Democrats, and a House and Senate in which the insurgent elements were making their presence felt, should delegate few investigations to a Federal Trade Commission under the chairmanship of W. E. Humphrey.[95] A portion of Mr. Humphrey's speech before the United States Chamber of Commerce in 1925 was indicative of the attitude of this Coolidge appointee.

[95] He was later noted for failing to see eye to eye with President Roosevelt.

Referring to the proposals by Senators LaFollette, Norris, and Shipstead for various investigations to be conducted by the Commission, he opinionated: " It is perfectly useless to take time to explain the purpose of these resolutions. It is clearly apparent that the primal motive in all of them is political—to advance the personal fortunes of some person, party, or class." [96] While it must be conceded that such a show of diametrically opposite viewpoints forms a compelling argument against delegation, so direct a conflict of philosophies is probably more singular than general. Moreover, a situation of this sort is usually short-lived. Although Congress, therefore, may be justified, during a transient period, in refusing to invite a slothful inquiry by delegating an investigation to a particular agency, it seems fair to say that such a distrust is only occasionally warranted. Furthermore, the case against delegation is weakened by the realization that Congress may at times have a choice among administrative agencies.

Perhaps the most important circumstance operating against the delegation of the inquisitorial investigations, however, is the breadth of the investigatory power of Congressional committees as compared to that of other agencies. Students may disagree as to the exact boundaries of the powers of a committee of the Senate or House. Little exception would be taken, however, to the general assertion that they are extensive. The courts, particularly in recent years, have hesitated to impose restraints on them. But, on the other hand, an administrative agency's authority, no matter how broad within a particular area, may not extend to other fields. Thus, when information was desired on the intricacies of the financing of the railroads, a resolution,[97] introduced by Senator Wheeler, directed an investigation by the Senate Committee on Interstate Commerce. The Senator, greeted by a barrage of questioning as to why the inquiry should not be conducted by the Interstate Commerce

[96] Quoted by Senator Norris, *Congressional Record*, 70th Cong., 1st Sess., p. 2955. Also see *New York Times*, May 21, 1925.

[97] S. Res. 71, 74th Cong., 1st Sess., May 20, 1935.

Commission, explained: " Under the law at the present time, as has been testified by members of the Commission, there is certain information which the Interstate Commerce Commission cannot obtain.   I wish to say . . . that we intend to work with the Commission and the Commission, as a matter of fact, will do practically all this work, but it is necessary to have this resolution adopted in order to reach some of the railroads' affiliates and holding companies." [98] Because a proposed investigation is not relevant to the functions of a regulatory commission, therefore, that commission may be without power to conduct the inquiry.[99]

The investigations which have been entrusted to administrative agencies have, moreover, encountered obstacles as a result of a doctrine that Congress cannot delegate its full power of

[98] *Congressional Record*, 74th Cong., 1st Sess., p. 7818, May 20, 1935. The accuracy of this contention was attested to later in a letter to Senator Wheeler by Joseph B. Eastman, a member of the Commission and the former Federal Coordinator of railroads: " To a considerable extent we might have conducted such an inquiry on our own account, but I am glad that your committee has undertaken it for these reasons: First. Our powers of inquiry are largely confined to the carriers, but these financial matters ramify into banking and holding company activities which your committee has powers to investigate but we have not." *Congressional Record*, 75th Cong., 1st Sess., p. 700, February 2, 1937.

[99] If, however, the Senate and House, by a joint resolution, request an investigation by a commission, they can, in the same resolution, confer " additional power " on the commission for the purposes of the particular investigation. Federal Trade Commission *v.* National Biscuit Co., 18 F. Supp. 667 (1937).

Since some investigations by the regulatory commissions have been challenged on the basis of the doctrine that these agencies cannot conduct inquiries which are outside of the interstate commerce field, it should be noted that Congress, by the public utility act of 1935 (49 Stat. 803) gave the Federal Power Commission the power to compel the intrastate as well as interstate power enterprises to submit certain information; sec. 311, for example, provides: " In order to secure information necessary or appropriate as a basis for recommending legislation, the Commission is authorized and directed to conduct investigations regarding the generation, transmission, distribution, and sale of electric energy, however produced, throughout the United States and its possessions, whether or not otherwise subject to the jurisdiction of the Commission . . ."

inquiry. The activities of the various agencies pursuant to investigation have, in the past, been substantially belabored by the decisions of the courts.[100] To a considerable extent, probing administrators have remained impotent in the face of recalcitrancy. The courts have, in general, tended to approve the investigations by commissions which concerned specific breaches of the laws administered by the commissions, or which were clearly necessary for the enforcement of these existing laws; but the courts have been less inclined to uphold inquiries that were conducted by the commissions for other purposes. Indeed, doubt has been expressed by one writer as to whether the commissions can search for facts other than those necessary for the enforcement of the laws.[101] Another student of the subject has concluded that, barring judicial or quasi-judicial investigations, only Congress or its committees can inquire into private affairs.[102] There is, however, a basis for the belief that the administrative agencies may be given ample power for the conduct of most of the inquiries which Congress wishes to be made. The recent experience of the Federal Trade Commission may be cited in support of this conclusion. In the event that Congress should adopt a policy of a more frequent delegation of its inquisitorial investigations, it seems likely that this Commission, because its field of activities is wide, would be one of the more useful probing tools. Although the Commission's inquiries have, in the past, been hampered by the courts, an analysis of the cases of recent years seems to lend support to the conclusion that the Commission's power to compel the production of papers and the giving of testimony is adequate for conducting broad investigations. The decision in Federal

---

[100] Harriman v. Interstate Commerce Commission, 211 U. S. 407 (1908), is frequently quoted to support the contention that a commission's power to investigate is strictly limited. See also Federal Trade Commission v. Baltimore Grain Products Co., 284 F. 886 (1922), and American Tobacco Co. v. Federal Trade Commission, 264 U. S. 298 (1924).

[101] Eberling, op. cit., p. 421.

[102] A. Langeluttig, "Constitutional Limitations on Administrative Power of Investigation," 28 Illinois Law Review 508 (1933).

Trade Commission *v.* Smith [103] was especially helpful. The investigation in question—the inquiry into the electric and gas public utilities [104]—was particularly significant. The effective way in which it was conducted furnishes convincing evidence that the Federal Trade Commission has sufficient power to make a thorough investigation of the type which has been characterized as inquisitorial. The Commission, encountering objections by the Electric Bond & Share Co. to the subpoenas *duces tecum* and to the questions which were asked in the hearings, applied for a writ of mandamus requiring the representatives of the corporation to answer the questions and to produce their operating expense ledgers and other papers. The District Court's opinion was so favorable to the Commission that the latter reported: " The examination of operating expenses of the Electric Bond & Share Co. was finally made, the company complying in all respects not only with this demand of the Commission but also with a great many others which had been held for a long time in abeyance." [105] That the consequences of the decision reached beyond one corporation is also attested by the further assertion that " This proceeding . . . appears to have had a very salutary effect in connection with the general conduct of the inquiry. . . . Thereafter even the most persistent refusals were overcome in all important matters." In the other instances in the period of this study when the courts were presented with questions as to the Federal Trade Commission's power to investigate pursuant to simple or joint resolutions of Congress, the decisions [106] also ran favorable to the

[103] 1 F. Supp. 247 (1932).

[104] S. Res. 83, 70th Cong., 1st Sess., February 13, 1928.

[105] *Summary Report* of the Federal Trade Commission, S. Doc. 92, 70th Cong., 1st Sess., part 72A, p. 19.

[106] In Federal Trade Commission *v.* Millers' National Federation, 47 F (2d) 428 (1931), the Court of Appeals of the District of Columbia declared invalid an injunction which was sought by a trade association to restrain the enforcement of subpoenas issued by the Commission in pursuance of an investigation into the control of prices in the flour and bread industries (S. Res. 163, 68th Cong., 1st Sess.).

The Commission was also supported by a District Court when, during its

Commission.[107] If, as the cases of the past decade seem to indicate, the regulatory commissions have, or may be granted, sufficient power to handle effectively the inquisitorial investigations which Congress might entrust to them, the reasoning against the advisability of more frequent delegation is materially weakened.

Moreover, one further thought should be added in support of delegation. In spite of any legal distinctions between the

investigation into the agricultural income (49 Stat. 929), it applied for a writ of mandamus to compel the National Biscuit Co. to answer questions relating to their sales. Federal Trade Commission v. National Biscuit Co., 18 F. Supp. 667 (1937).

[107] An analysis of the instances in which the inquiries of the Securities and Exchange Commission have been challenged show that, in general, the investigatory activities of this Commission have been sustained by the courts. Most of the cases have related only to the Commission's power to investigate for the purpose of ascertaining whether violations of the acts which it administers have occurred or are threatened. See Consolidated Mines of California v. S. E. C., 97 F (2) 704 (1938); Newfield v. Ryan, 91 F (2d) 700 (1937); and McMann v. S. E. C., 87 F (2d) 377 (1937). In Jones v. S. E. C., 298 U. S. 1 (1936), however, the Supreme Court refused to allow the Commission to continue an investigation as to the validity of a securities' registration statement after the registrant had withdrawn his statement; although the Commission has the power to conduct investigations which it thinks necessary and proper for the enforcement of the securities act (sec. 19b), Justice Sutherland, who delivered the opinion, insisted that "The difficulty with that is that the investigation was undertaken for the declared purpose of determining whether a stop order should issue."

The only Congressional requests for investigations by the Securities and Exchange Commission were contained in the securities and exchange act of 1934 and the public utility act of 1935. The one serious question of the power of the Commission to conduct these inquiries came from Frederck T. Fisher, a stockholder in the Equity Corporation, who challenged the validity of subpoenas which the Commission had issued in connection with its investigation of the investment trusts (sec. 30 of the public utility act, 49 Stat. 837). The subpoenas did not require the production of any documentary evidence but merely directed Fisher and the officers and directors of the Equity Corporation to appear and testify. Justice Bailey of the Supreme Court of the District of Columbia denied Mr. Fisher's motions for preliminary injunctions on the ground of a want of equity. Fisher v. Landis and Fisher v. The Equity Corporation; see New York Times, August 11, 1936, and the Third Annual Report of the Securities and Exchange Commission (1937), p. 52.

powers of the commissions and of Congressional committees, the investigatory authority of the former is probably sufficient for conducting the average inquiry. This inference is warranted partly because, as has been suggested, the more common attitude on the part of the persons who are investigated is not one of battling but rather of submission. In the majority of the investigations, the subpoena is not essential; it is, moreover, sometimes employed only at the request of a witness, who hesitates to supply any information without a clearly evidenced obligation. Because subpoenas often make news, the frequency and necessity of their use are exaggerated. Furthermore, the administrators' power for conducting an inquiry may be adequate because the investigators' adroitness forms a substitute for a specific authority. Thus, a method indirectly may bring results. One inquiring body, for example, having been refused an admission to some business offices for the purpose of a general inspection of the files, nevertheless was able to unearth an abundance of pertinent material in those files by issuing specific subpoenas for letters referred to in the correspondence found in other offices where the committee had an unlimited privilege to search. The tricks of the trade are many, and they vary and multiply from investigation to investigation as new obstructions are erected. Occasionally they perhaps border on the extreme; thus, one agency, as a last resort, was successful in smoking out information by means of requesting papers which were publicly purported to be more incriminating than they actually were. There seems to be little exaggeration in the statement made to the writer by a member of one of the regulatory commissions that, although the legal obstacles may some times cause inconvenient delays to the investigators, " a smart man can get all the information needed either for a committee or a commission."

TWO STEPS TO AN INVESTIGATION.   Despite the array of opposition, a more frequent delegation by Congress of its inquiries seems to be desirable. Some investigations, admittedly, may be best conducted by Congressional committees. Thus, as has been suggested, a considerable portion of the inquiries which are necessary in connection with the supervision of the Executive probably should be undertaken by committees of the House or Senate. Indeed, in every field of inquiry, there is a need, on some occasions, for an investigating device that is composed of legislators. A number of inquiries, however, may be entrusted to other agencies; when this action is taken, an investigation may be envisioned as a procedure of two distinct steps: the first, an impartial unearthing and assembling of all the pertinent facts; the second, the utilization of those facts. Whatever agency is responsible for the first, it should be allowed to proceed without any influence from the legislators. Its duty would be to seek out the facts (public hearings sometimes might be required to insure that the persons under investigation have a chance to air their case), to present them in orderly form, and to draw conclusions and recommendations based on this information. To the Senators and Representatives the task would remain of applying the facts.

The principal problem of such a division of labor would probably be to overcome the danger that the reports would receive scant attention and would rapidly find their way to unused files. Some means would have to be found of bridging the conceivable gap between the investigative and the legislative activity. The conduct of open hearings by Congressional committees on the reports of the fact finders would be a possible solution. The resolutions which authorize the investigations could specify an agency outside of Congress to collect and sift the information, and at the same time could designate a standing or select committee to which the report should be submitted. It would generally be the duty of the latter group to hold public hearings. Since the fact-finding body may already have pursued this procedure, however, the Congressional committee might well confine itself in the main to the taking of oral evidence from those who were responsible for the report. A primary aim of these final hearings would relate to social leverage; the legislators would thus retain a full opportunity to educate the public and to arouse general opinion. The hearings, therefore, would provide an instrument by which Congress could match the advantageous publicity that attends the investigatory reports issued in company with Presidential statements. At the same time, the Senators or Representatives could utilize the hearings for clarifying and to some extent verifying the information in the report. Additional witnesses might be called to help fill any disclosed gaps, although care should be taken to avoid a mere rehash. On occasion, the Congressmen might wish to hear a witness who appeared to have an authentic complaint that the persons who collected the information did not act impartially. The committee would draft its report to Congress—perhaps in the form of a bill—after this public investigation of the investigators.

The fundamental legitimate end of Congressional investigations would seem to be, in the final analysis, an unbiased uncovering of all the facts on a given subject. In actual practice, however, the information which is unearthed is always colored by the ideas in the minds of those who dig. The two step procedure here outlined is offered as no panacea. It would seem, however, to foster a more rigid objectivity than when Congressmen perform both steps. If it is borne in mind that the investigatory process by its very nature must remain flexible, it seems desirable that the legislators should more commonly lay aside their plows and leave to others the turning of facts and the preparation of fields for Congressional working.

BIBLIOGRAPHY

GOVERNMENT PUBLICATIONS

Advisory Committee on Education, *Report of the Committee* (1938).

Attorney General of the United States, *Annual Report* (1936).

Cannon, Clarence, *Cannon's Precedents of the House of Representatives* (1936), vol. 6.

Commission on Industrial Relations in Great Britain, *Report* (1938).

Committee on Economic Security, *Report to the President* (1935).

Congressional Record, 56th to 75th Congresses.

Federal Trade Commission, *Annual Reports* (1929 to 1938).

Federal Trade Commission, *Summary Report*, S. Doc. 92, 70th Cong., 1st Sess., part 72A.

Great Plains Committee, *The Future of the Great Plains* (1937).

National Resources Committee, *The Problems of a Changing Population* (1938).

National Resources Committee, *Public Works Planning* (1936).

National Resources Committee, *Regional Factors in National Planning and Development* (1935).

President's Committee on Administrative Management, *Report with Special Studies* (1937).

President's Committee on Crop Insurance, *Report and Recommendations* (1936).

President's Committee on Farm Tenancy, *Report of the President's Committee* (1937).

President's Committee of Industrial Analysis, *The National Recovery Administration* (1937).

Securities and Exchange Commission, *Annual Reports* (1935 to 1938).

U. S. Congress, House of Representatives, Hearings of Committees.

U. S. Congress, House of Representatives, *Rules*.

U. S. Congress, House of Representatives, Reports of Committees.

U. S. Congress, Senate, Hearings of Committees.

U. S. Congress, Senate, Reports of Committees.

U. S. Congress, Senate, *Senate Manual*.

BOOKS

Beard, Charles A., *The Devil Theory of War* (New York, The Vanguard Press, 1936).

Chamberlain, Joseph P., *Legislative Processes, National and State* (New York, D. Appleton-Century, 1936).

Clokie, H. M., and Robinson, J. W., *Royal Commissions of Inquiry* (Stanford University, Stanford University Press, 1937).

Dimock, Marshall E., *Congressional Investigating Committees* (Baltimore, Johns Hopkins Press, 1929).

Eberling, Ernest J., *Congressional Investigations* (New York, 1928).

Frankfurter, Felix, *The Public and Its Government* (New Haven, Yale University Press, 1930).

Haynes, George H., *The Senate of the United States* (Boston, Houghton Mifflin Co., 1938).

Holcombe, A. N., *Government in a Planned Democracy* (New York, W. W. Norton & Co., 1935).

Huberman, Leo, *The Labor Spy Racket* (New York, Modern Age Books, 1937).

Lorwin, Lewis L., *Advisory Economic Councils* (Washington, The Brookings Institution, 1931).

Mansfield, Harvey C., *The Comptroller General* (New Haven, Yale University Press, 1939).

Mitchell, E. Y., *Kicked In and Kicked Out of the President's Little Cabinet* (Washington, The Andrew Jackson Press, 1936).

Moley, Raymond, *Politics and Criminal Prosecution* (New York, Minton, Balch & Co., 1929).

Myers, W. S., and Newton, W. H., *The Hoover Administration* (New York, C. Scribner's Sons, 1936).

Reynolds, Mary F. Trackett, *Interdepartmental Committees in the National Administration* (New York, Columbia University Press, 1939).

Rogers, Lindsay, *The American Senate* (New York, A. A. Knopf, 1926).

Rosen, S. McKee, *Political Process* (New York, Harper & Brothers, 1935).

Walker, Harvey, *Law Making in the United States* (New York, The Ronald Press, 1934).

Webb, Sidney and Beatrice, *Methods of Social Study* (London, Longmans, 1932).

Willoughby, W. F., *Principles of Legislative Organization and Administration* (Washington, The Brookings Institution, 1934).

ARTICLES

Bell, Laird, " Probes," 160 *Atlantic Monthly* 23 (1937).

Bent, Silas, " Mr. Hoover's Sins of Commissions," 90 *Scribner's* 9 (1931).

Black, Hugo L., " Inside a Senate Investigation," 172 *Harpers* 275 (1936).

Boston University Law Review, Note on Hearst *v.* Black, 17 *Boston University Law Review* 141 (1937).

Colclough, O. S., " Security Exchange Commission's Power of Search," 3 *George Washington Law Review* 356 (1935).

Columbia Law Review, Note on Strawn *v.* Western Union, 36 *Columbia Law Review* 841 (1936).

Coudert, Frederic R., " Congressional Inquisitions *v.* Individual Liberty," 15 *Virginia Law Review* 537 (1929).

Cousens, Theodore W., " The Purposes and Scope of Investigations Under Legislative Authority," 26 *Georgetown Law Journal* 905 (1938).

Dorr, Harold M., "A Legislative Council for Michigan," 28 *American Political Science Review* 270 (1934).

Fisher, W. W., " Delegation of Legislative Investigating Power to Administrative Bodies," 14 *Texas Law Review* 385 (1936).

Flynn, John T., Notes, 89 *New Republic* 74 (1936).
——, "Senate Inquisitors and Private Rights," 161 *Harpers* 357 (1930).
Frankfurter, Felix, "Hands Off the Investigations," 38 *New Republic* 329 (1924).
Gallagher, Hubert R., "Legislative Councils," 24 *National Municipal Review* 147 (1935).
Galloway, George B., "Investigations, Governmental," *Encyclopaedia of the Social Sciences*, vol. 8, p. 251.
——, "The Investigative Function of Congress," 21 *American Political Science Review* 47 (1927).
Gose, Jack, "The Limits of Congressional Investigating Power," 10 *Washington Law Review* 61 and 138 (1935).
Gosnell, H. F., "British Royal Commissions of Inquiry," 49 *Political Science Quarterly* 84 (1934).
Guild, Frederick H., "Achievements of the Kansas Legislative Council," 29 *American Political Science Review* 636 (1935).
Hamilton, Bryce L., "The Inquisitorial Power of Congress," 23 *American Bar Association Journal* 511 (1937).
Handler, Milton, "Constitutionality of Investigations by the Federal Trade Commission," 28 *Columbia Law Review* 708 and 905 (1928).
Harvard Law Review, Note on Jurney v. MacCracken, 48 *Harvard Law Review* 848 (1935).
Kelly, Fred C., "Government by Test-Tube," 49 *Current History* 35 (1939).
Landis, James M., "Constitutional Limitations on the Congressional Power of Investigation," 40 *Harvard Law Review* 153 (1926).
Langeluttig, A., "Constitutional Limitations on Administrative Power of Investigation," 28 *Illinois Law Review* 508 (1933).
Lippmann, Walter, "The Senate Inquisition," 84 *Forum* 129 (1930).
MacChesney, Brunson, "Further Developments in 'Disclosure' Under the Securities Act," 33 *Illinois Law Review* 145 (1938).
Michigan Law Review, Notes on Federal Trade Commission v. National Biscuit Co., and Hearst v. Black, 35 *Michigan Law Review* 1380 and 1383 (1937).
Rogers, Lindsay, "Parliamentary Commissions in France," 38 *Political Science Quarterly* 413 and 602 (1923).
Rogers, Lindsay, and Dittmar, W. R., "The Reichswirtschaftsrat: De Mortius," 50 *Political Science Quarterly* 481 (1935).
Shull, Charles W., "Congressional Investigations and Contempts," 63 *United States Law Review* 326 (1929).
——, "Legislative Contempt—An Auxiliary Power of Congress," 8 *Temple Law Quarterly* 198 (1933).
Smith, T. V., "Illinois Calls on Kansas," 10 *State Government* 252 (1937).
Stradley, Leighton P., "Constitutionality of Compulsory Statistical Reports of the Federal Trade Commission," 76 *University of Pennsylvania Law Review* 19 (1927).
United States Law Week, Note on Strawn v. Western Union Telegraph Co., 3 *United States Law Week* 646 (1936).

Virginia Law Review, Note on Newfield *v.* Ryan, 24 *Virginia Law Review* 201 (1937).

Wigmore, John H., " The Federal Senate as a Fifth Wheel," 24 *Illinois Law Review* 89 (1929).

Yale Law Journal, "Investigatory Powers of the Securities and Exchange Commission," 44 *Yale Law Journal* 819 (1935).

Ziegler, Martha J., "Legislators Work Between Sessions," 10 *State Government* 236 (1937).

Miscellaneous

Parliamentary Papers, 1912-13, vol. VIII, "Special Report (no. 515) from the Select Committee on Marconi's Wireless Telegraph Company, Limited, Agreement."

Parliamentary Papers, 1910, vol. LVIII, "Report (Cmd. 5235) of the Departmental Committee on the Procedure of Royal Commissions."

Perkins, James A., *Congress Investigates Our Foreign Relations* (Unpublished dissertation, Princeton, 1937).

Cases Cited

American Tobacco Co. *v.* Federal Trade Commission, 264 U. S. 298 (1924).

Barry *v.* United States, 279 U. S. 597 (1929).

Burroughs and Cannon *v.* United States, 290 U. S. 534 (1934).

Consolidated Mines of California *v.* Securities and Exchange Commission, 97 F (2d) 704 (1938).

Fisher *v.* The Equity Corporation, and Fisher *v.* Landis (Unreported—see *New York Times,* August 11, 1936).

Federal Trade Commission *v.* Baltimore Grain Products Co., 284 F. 886 (1922).

Federal Trade Commission *v.* Millers' National Federation, 47 F (2d) 428 (1931).

Federal Trade Commission *v.* National Biscuit Co., 18 F. Supp. 667 (1937).

Federal Trade Commission *v.* Smith, 1 F. Supp. 247 (1932).

Harriman *v.* Interstate Commerce Commission, 211 U. S. 407 (1908).

Hearst *v.* Black, 87 F (2d) 68 (1936).

In re Chapman, 166 U. S. 661 (1897).

Jones *v.* Securities and Exchange Commission, 298 U. S. 1 (1936).

Jurney *v.* MacCracken, 294 U. S. 125 (1935).

Kilbourn *v.* Thompson, 103 U. S. 168 (1881).

Marshall *v.* Gordon, 243 U. S. 521 (1917).

McGrain *v.* Daugherty, 273 U. S. 135 (1927).

McMann *v.* Securities and Exchange Commission, 87 F (2d) 377 (1937).

Newberry *v.* United States, 256 U. S. 232 (1921).

Newfield *v.* Ryan, 91 F (2d) 700 (1937).

Railroad Labor Board *v.* Robertson, 3 F (2d) 488 (1925).

Reed *v.* The County Commissioners of Delaware County, Pennsylvania, 277 U. S. 376 (1928).

Seymour *v.* United States, 77 F (2d) 577 (1935).

Sinclair *v.* United States, 279 U. S. 263 (1929).

Standard Computing Scale Co. *v.* Farrell, 249 U. S. 571 (1919).

Strawn *v.* Western Union Telegraph Co. (Unreported—see 3 *United States Law Week* 646, and *New York Times*, March 12, 1936).

Townsend *v.* United States, 95 F (2d) 352 (1938).

United States *v.* Norris, 300 U. S. 564 (1937).

INDEX